VEGAN DESSERTS

Sumptuous Sweets for Every Season

HANNAH KAMINSKY

Skyhorse Publishing

Skyhorse Publishing books may be purchased in bulk at special discounts for sales promotion, corporate gifts, fund-raising, or educational purposes. Special editions can also be created to specifications. For details, contact the Special Sales Department, Skyhorse Publishing, 307 West 36th Street, 11th Floor, New York, NY 10018 or info@skyhorsepublishing.com.

Skyhorse® and Skyhorse Publishing® are registered trademarks of Skyhorse Publishing, Inc.®, a Delaware corporation.

www.skyhorsepublishing.com

10 9 8 7 6 5 4 3 2 1

Paperback ISBN: 978-1-63450-390-7

Library of Congress Cataloging-in-Publication Data is on file.

Printed in China

CONTENTS

INTRO

There's no question about it—food made with ingredients at their prime and in season tastes best. Deceptively simple in concept, but remarkably more complicated than most would like to admit, there's so much more to take into consideration than just the range of produce available at the nearest grocery store. Fresh, local produce, at the peak of ripeness, is at the heart of seasonal eating, providing incomparable flavors that simply cannot be replicated with any amount of sugar, salt, or baking extracts ever created by man. Without a solid source of these staple ingredients, any baker can only hope to create desserts on par with the norm, never anything particularly spectacular. I don't know about you, but no almond extract that has ever passed my lips holds a candle to real whole almonds. It does a fairly decent job of imitation, but almond it is not. Thus the greatest challenge when it comes to creating showstopping dishes, sweet or savory, is less about the preparation of food and more about learning to respect and let the food be, so it can shine through with its true essence.

All that said, eating and baking seasonally needn't be difficult, and it certainly shouldn't be seen as a tiresome chore. Just go with your gut, explore your options, and eat what looks good. Mother Nature is a fickle woman, and herein lies the first great stumbling block to baking and cooking enlightenment. Availability will vary greatly based on your climate, location, and of course the current season, so while raspberries first poke their timid red heads out from the bushes around early to mid-August for me, they'll have already been on the scene in California practically long enough to call themselves permanent residents. In cases such as these, other berries could very easily be used instead of those illusive raspberries, and in a pinch, frozen can often make an adequate stand-in. Just because we all know that the fresh will taste better when they're abundant in the late summer doesn't mean we can always stop those midwinter berry cravings! There's no need to be militant about this stuff either, which is why the following recipes should truly be considered more as guidelines than rules.

Though baking is less forgiving than cooking when it comes to making substitutions, there's still plenty of room for interpretation in each and every formula. I've provided some helpful hints when possible, indicating areas where key fruits and somewhat obscure ingredients can be swapped for something that might be easier to come by, but don't be afraid to get in there and experiment for yourself. Make the recipe once as written to know how it *should* come out, and then go crazy, take a risk, consider yourself a mad baking scientist! Since I never had formal training myself, this is exactly how I learned to hone my skills, gain appreciation for the alchemy that occurs every time you put a cake in the oven and watch it rise to incredible heights, and generally become passionate about this creative kitchen craft. The worst thing that a baker can do, experienced or fresh in the field, is to become too rigid with their recipes. It's only food, after all, and playing with it to make something even sweeter should always be fun!

When approaching seasonal desserts, too few people consider the calendar itself. By that, I don't mean the general months and times of harvest, but the actual man-made calendar, complete with holidays, events, and special occasions woven in. So many sweet treats are prepared in honor of times of celebration, and are inextricably linked to those particular times of the year, regardless of the growing schedule. So many of my fondest Hanukkah and Halloween memories revolve around desserts of some sort, and to ignore these gems based solely on their ingredients would be a grave oversimplification of the whole concept of seasonality. Just like rhubarb, these moments come but once every year, and are to be savored to the greatest extent possible when they finally arrive. That's why you may stumble across a few recipes that have you scratching your head as to why they made the cut, but bear with me. Irresistible recipes are about more than fresh fruit—food always tastes better when made with joy, care, patience, and just a pinch of good humor.

INGREDIENTS GLOSSARY

Active Dry Yeast

Found either in little packets or larger bulk tins, this is baking yeast that has been dried and essentially "put to sleep." To wake it up, it must be soaked in warm (but not hot!) liquid for a few minutes until frothy, before adding the yeast into most doughs. Rapid rise yeast is essentially the same, but doesn't require the soaking step and will leaven baked goods in about half the time of traditional active dry. However, what you sacrifice for the speed is flavor, so I never purchase rapid rise. Stored in a cool place like the fridge, dry yeast can keep for nearly a year. Each little packet contains approximately 2¼ teaspoons or ¼ ounce of yeast.

Agave Nectar

Derived from the same plant as tequila but far less potent, agave is the sweet syrup at the core of cacti. It is available in both light and dark varieties; the dark possesses a more nuanced, complex, and somewhat floral flavor, while the light tends to provide only a clean sweetness. Unrefined, agave nectar has a much lower glycemic index than many traditional granulated sweeteners, and is therefore consumed by some diabetics in moderation. Any health food or natural food store worth its stuff should readily stock agave nectar.

Agar (Agar-Agar)

Known also as kanten, agar is a gelatinous substance made out of seaweed. It is a perfect substitute for traditional gelatin, which is extracted from the collagen within animals' connective tissues and obviously extremely not vegan. Agar comes in both powdered and flaked form. I prefer to use the powder because it is easier to incorporate smoothly into puddings, faster to thicken, and measures gram for gram like standard gelatin. However, if you can only find the flakes, just whiz them in a spice grinder for a few minutes and, viola, instant agar powder! Agar can be found in Asian markets and some health food stores.

All-Purpose Flour

While wonderful flours can be made from all sorts of grains, beans, nuts, and seeds, the gold standard in everyday baking would be all-purpose. Falling somewhere between cake flour and bread flour, all-purpose flour has the ability to create light desserts which still have substance. It is therefore used most often in my recipes, and stocked as one of my pantry staples. All-purpose flour may be labeled in stores as unbleached white flour or simply "plain flour."

Almond Meal/Flour

Almond flour is simply the end result of grinding down raw almonds into a fine powder; almond meal is generally just a bit coarser. To make your own, just throw a pound or so of completely unadulterated almonds into your food processor and let the machine work its magic. If you opt to stock up and save some for later, be sure to store the freshly ground almond flour within an airtight container in the refrigerator or freezer. Due to their high oil content, ground nuts can go rancid fairly quickly. To cut down on labor and save a little time, almond flour or meal can be purchased in bulk from natural food grocers.

Apple Cider Vinegar

As with oil, vinegar can be made from all sorts of fruit, grains, and roots, which all create unique flavor profiles and chemical compositions in the finished product. Thinking along these lines, apple cider vinegar could be considered the olive oil of vinegars; flavorful, useful, and an all-around great thing to have on hand. Regular white wine vinegar or the other standard options would certainly work, but the distinctive "twang" of apple cider vinegar rounds out baked goods so perfectly, and it is so easy to find—why wouldn't you use it? Hunt around the oil and salad dressing aisles in your local supermarket, where you should have no problem securing a bottle.

Arrowroot Powder/Flour

Thanks to arrowroot you can thicken sauces, puddings, and mousses with ease. This white powder is very similar to kudzu and is often compared to other starchy flours. However, arrowroot is so fine that it produces much smoother, creamier results, and is less likely to stick together and form large glutinous lumps. In a pinch, an equal measure of either cornstarch or potato starch can make for adequate substitutes, but I highly recommend seeking out arrowroot. Most megamarts have one or two brands to choose from tucked in among the flours in the baking aisle.

Black Cocoa Powder

What do you get when you oxidize Dutch-processed cocoa powder to the extreme? Black cocoa, of course! Dark as coal, it certainly lives up to its name and produces amazing jet-black color in baked goods. However, it has a much lower fat content than standard cocoa, and should therefore be used sparingly to avoid altering the texture of your baked goods. I rarely use black cocoa because it is difficult to find and more expensive than the alternative. Nonetheless, if you wish to create breathtaking chocolate desserts, black cocoa will never fail to impress. You can hunt it down at some tea or spice specialty shops, but if all else fails, a search online should prove fruitful. Feel free to substitute regular Dutch-processed cocoa for an equally tasty, if comparatively pale, dessert.

Brown Rice Syrup

Caramel colored and thick like honey, brown rice syrup is a natural sweetener that is produced via the fermentation of brown rice. It is actually less sweet than granulated sugar, adding a wholesome complexity to baked goods. The deep flavor of brown rice syrup is best cast in supporting roles, complementing other aspects of the dish without taking center stage. Brown rice syrup can be found in health food stores across the map, but corn syrup will make a suitable substitute, if you are unable to find it locally.

Cacao Nibs

Also known as raw chocolate, cacao nibs are unprocessed cacao nuts, simply broken up into smaller pieces. Much more bitter and harsh than the sweet, mellow chocolate found in bars or chips, it is often used for texture and accent flavor in most desserts. Sometimes it can be found coated in sugar to soften its inherent acidity, but for baking, you want the plain, raw version if possible. Seek out bags of cacao nibs in health food stores; if you're really lucky, you may be able to find them in the bulk bins of well-stocked specialty stores.

Chestnut Flour

Once unheard of in the everyday consumer kitchen, the popularity of chestnut flour is now on the fast track upward, thanks to the increasing awareness of celiac disease. Made simply of dry, ground chestnuts, it's naturally gluten free and packed with nutty, slightly sweet flavor, making it an ideal flour alternative in many baked goods. I tend to choose it based on flavor alone, but if using it to replace standard wheat flour, you'll want to use a blend of other gluten-free flours and starches since it doesn't have quite enough heft to stand all on its own. Chestnut flour can be found in abundance online, and often in the baking section of health food stores.

Chocolate

Chocolate is chocolate, right? One would assume so, but many name brands that prefer quantity to quality would beg to differ. Obviously, white and milk chocolate are out of the picture, yet some dark and semisweet chocolates still don't make the vegan cut. Even those that claim to be "70 percent cacao solids, extraspecial dark" may have milk solids or butterfat lurking within. Don't buy the hype or the filler! Stay vigilant and check labels for milk-based ingredients, as unadulterated chocolate is far superior.

Chocolate Crème-Filled Sandwich Cookies

As America's favorite cookie, it is no surprise that the Oreo would come up sooner or later on this list. While the original Oreo is now changing its ways to take out the trans fats and animal products, there are many other options that are even more ethically acceptable. Newman's Own makes an excellent organic version that tastes just like the cookies you might remember from your childhood. Plus, along with some exciting flavor variations, Newman-O's (as they are called) can even be found in a wheat-free format! Any Oreo-like cocoa wafers with a vegan crème filling will do, so it is up to your own discretion as to which brand you would like to endorse.

Coconut Milk

When called for in this book, I'm referring to regular full-fat coconut milk. In most cases, light coconut milk cannot be substituted without detrimental effects to flavor and texture. Especially when it comes to frozen desserts, that fat is necessary for a smooth, creamy mouth feel, and of course a richer taste. Plain coconut milk is found canned in the ethnic foods aisle of the grocery store. You can make it yourself from fresh coconut meat, but for use in baked goods, it's honestly not worth the expense or effort.

Confectioner's Sugar

Otherwise known as powdered sugar, icing sugar, or 10x sugar, confectioner's sugar is a very finely ground version of standard white sugar, often with a touch of starch included to prevent clumping. There are many vegan options on the market, so just keep your eyes open and you will likely find a good supply. Of course, you can make your own confectioner's sugar by powdering 1 cup of granulated sugar with 1 tablespoon of cornstarch in your food processor or spice grinder. Simply blend the sugar and cornstarch on the highest speed for about 2 minutes, allowing the dust to settle before opening your machine up—unless you want to inhale a cloud of sugar!

Dried Pomegranate Arils

Dried pomegranate arils can be a bit tricky to find in your average grocery store, but they're a snap to make at home. Just dehydrate 1 or 2 pomegranates' worth of cleaned and separated arils for 2–4 hours, or bake at the lowest temperature possible, for about 1 hour, stirring frequently.

Ener-G Egg Replacer

Although I'm typically resistant to calling for brand name mixes such as the powdered egg replacer indicated here, it simply isn't possible to make some of the more delicate (and traditionally egg white-based) cookies and pastry with anything else. If you want your vegan meringues and macaroons, you'll just have to bite the bullet and buy a box. It's a small price to pay for creating the "impossible" vegan meringue, if you ask me. Ener-G is available online and in select health food stores.

Flavor Extracts

In most cases, I try to stay as far away from extracts as possible, because they are all too often artificial, insipid, and a poor replacement for the real thing. However, real vanilla and almond are my two main exceptions, as high-quality extracts from the actual sources are readily available in most markets. Just make sure to avoid any bottles that contain sugar, corn syrup, colors, or chemical stabilizers in addition to your flavor of choice. For some of the more unusual extracts, if your supermarket searches end up unsuccessful, the Internet will never let you down.

Flaxseeds

Ground flaxseeds make an excellent vegan egg replacer when combined with water. One tablespoon of the whole seeds produces approximately 2 tablespoons of the ground powder. While you can purchase preground flax meal in many stores, I prefer to grind the flaxseeds fresh for each recipe, as they tend to go rancid rather quickly once broken down. Not to mention, it takes mere seconds to powder your own flaxseeds in a spice grinder! If you do opt to purchase flax meal instead, be sure to store the powder in your refrigerator or freezer until you are ready to use it. These tiny seeds can be found in bulk bins and prepackaged in the baking aisle of natural food stores.

Garbanzo (Chickpea) Flour

Gaining in popularity as a versatile gluten-free flour, garbanzo flour is just as you might imagine; nothing but dried, ground chickpeas! Although it is now used primarily in baking to substitute for wheat flours and to add a certain density to cakes or cookies, it can also be cooked with water like polenta and either eaten as a hot porridge or let set overnight in a baking dish, sliced, and then fried to make what is called chickpea panisse. Just be warned that eaten raw (if, say, someone decided to sample raw cookie batter that contains garbanzo flour), it is very bitter and unpleasant.

Garbanzo flour should be readily available in most grocery stores in the baking or natural foods section, but if you have a powerful blender like a Vita-Mix (see Kitchen Toys and Tools) with a dry grinding container, you can make your own from dried, split chickpeas (also known as chana dal). Process 2 cups of legumes at a time, and use the plunger to keep things moving. Once finely ground, let the mixture sit for a few minutes before removing the lid of the container so that the dust can settle.

Graham Cracker Crumbs

When I first went searching for vegan graham crackers, I was appalled by my lack of options. Why every brand in sight needed to include honey was beyond me. So, what is a hungry vegan baker to do in a tight situation like this? Keep on looking, of course. Concealed among the rest, and often in natural foods stores, there are a few brands that exclude all animal products. You can of course make your own and avoid a mad goose chase, following the recipe on page 229. Once you secure your crackers, you have two options to turn them into crumbs. For a coarse, more varied crumb, toss them into a sturdy plastic bag and just go at it with a rubber mallet or rolling pin! To achieve a fine, even crumb, grind them down in your food processor or spice grinder in batches, and you will have a perfect powder in no time.

Graham Flour

Most commonly found in the form of crackers, graham flour is simply a fancy type of wheat flour. It is made from a process that separates all parts of the wheat kernel itself and recombines them in different proportions. For reasons beyond my grasp, this particular flour is not sold in all countries. If you are having a hard time getting your hands on some and don't mind an end product with a slightly different texture, regular old whole wheat flour can be substituted. Of course, you may be able to locate graham flour online and save yourself the worry altogether.

Granulated Sugar

Yes, plain old regular white sugar. Surprised to see this basic sweetener here? It's true that all sugar (beet or cane) is derived from plant sources and therefore vegan by nature. However, there are some sneaky things going on behind the scenes in big corporations these days. Some cane sugar is filtered using bone char, a very nonvegan process, but it will never be specified on any labels. If you're not sure about the brand that you typically buy, your best bet is to contact the manufacturer directly and ask.

To bypass this problem, many vegans purchase unbleached cane sugar. While it is a suitable substitute, unbleached cane sugar does have a higher molasses content than white sugar, so it has more of a brown sugarlike flavor and tends to produce desserts that are denser. Luckily, there are a few caring companies that go through great pains to ensure the purity of their sugar products, such as Florida Crystals and Amalgamated Sugar Company, the suppliers to White Satin, Fred Meyer, Western Family, and Parade. I typically opt for one of these vegan sugar brands to get the best results. You can often find appropriate sugar in health food store bulk bins these days to save some money, but as always, verify the source before forking over the cash. As sugar can be a touchy vegan subject, it is best to use your own judgment when considering which brand to purchase.

Liquid Pectin

Typically derived from fruits, this is a thickener that is most commonly used in jams or jellies. Be aware that liquid pectin and powdered pectin have very different gelling properties and cannot be used interchangeably. I personally tend to favor Certo brand because it's widely available and very reliable. Liquid pectin can be found in the baking aisle of most grocery stores, near the pudding mixes.

Maple Syrup

One of my absolute favorite sweeteners, there is simply no substitute for real 100 percent maple syrup. The flavor is like nothing else out there, and I have yet to meet a single brand of pancake syrup that could even come close. Of course, this incredible indulgence does come at a hefty price, and the costs only continue to rise as the years go by and fewer people care to make maple syrup the old-fashioned way. Though it would be absolute sacrilege to use anything but authentic grade B maple syrup on pancakes or waffles in my house, I will sometimes bend the rules in recipes where there isn't such a prominent flavor in order to save some money. In these instances, I'll substitute with a maple-agave blend, which still carries the flavor from the actual source, but bulks it up with an equal dose of agave for sweetening power.

Matcha/Maccha Powder

Perhaps one of my all-time favorite flavorings, matcha is a very high-quality powdered green tea. It is used primarily in Japanese tea ceremonies and can have an intense, complex, and bitter taste when used in large amounts. Contrary to what many new bakers think, this is not the same as the green tea leaves you'll find in megamart tea bags! Those are vastly inferior in the flavor department, and real matcha is ground much finer. There are many levels of quality, with each step up in grade carrying a higher price tag. Because it can become quite pricey, I would suggest buying a medium grade, which should be readily available at any specialty tea store. When translated directly from Japanese, the spelling is maccha, but the typical English spelling is matcha. Whichever way the package is labeled, you will still find green tea powder within.

Non-Dairy Margarine

It is a basic kitchen staple at its core, but good margarine can actually be quite elusive if you do not know what to look for. Some name brands contain whey or other milk derivatives, while others conceal the elusive animal-derived vitamin D3, so be alert when scanning ingredient labels. For ease, I prefer to use stick margarines, such as Earth Balance or Willow Run. Never try to substitute spreadable margarine from a tub! These varieties have much more water to allow them to spread while cold, and will thus bake differently. I always use unsalted margarine unless otherwise noted, but you are welcome to use salted as long as you omit ¼—½ teaspoon of salt per stick (½ cup) of margarine used in the recipe. Overly salted food is one of the first flaws that diners pick up on, so take care with your seasoning!

Non-Dairy Milk

Unless explicitly specified, any type of vegan milk substitute will work just fine here. My typical pick for baking is unsweetened soymilk, simply because it's the easiest to find, neutral in flavor, and one of the less expensive options, but I'm also quite fond of unsweetened almond milk. Don't forget the whole wide world of options out there; between hemp, oat, rice, hazelnut, coconut, and more, there's a lot to choose from!

Red Wine

While I don't actually drink, I can tell you that if your wine isn't something you'd want in a glass, it's not something you'd want in a cake or sorbet either. Avoid so-called cooking wines and just go with something moderately priced, and on the sweeter side to complement the dessert that it's going into. Don't be afraid to ask for help when you go shopping; the people who work at wine stores tend to have good advice about these things! Be vigilant and do your homework though, because not all wines are vegan. Shockingly, some are filtered through isinglass, which is actually made from fish bladders! So, to avoid a fishy brew, double-check brands on http://www.barnivore.com.

Ricemellow Crème

Remember that old childhood favorite, Marshmallow Fluff? Well, Ricemellow Crème is its vegan equivalent, void of animal-based gelatins and refined sugars. Light, fluffy, and unlike anything else currently on the market, I have yet to find a suitable vegan alternative for Ricemellow Crème. It can be purchased at most natural food stores, or via online purveyors.

Salt

The importance of salt in desserts cannot be overstated. It's that spark that makes flavors pop, and balances out a bit of the sweetness that might otherwise overwhelm the palate. Unless otherwise noted, I use regular old table salt (finely ground) in baking. Kosher salt can be a fun addition in places where you really want the salt to stand out, like in chocolate chip cookies, but be careful not to overdo it; there's a fine line between salted and downright salty.

Soy (or Coconut) Creamer

Vegan creamer based on soy or coconut is a thicker liquid than regular nondairy milk, though it is not an equal substitute for dairy-based heavy cream. While it adds richness and moisture to cakes and creamy spreads, vegan creamers lack the proper ratio of proteins necessary to make whipped cream. Rather, it consists primarily of sugars, and consequently boasts a sweeter taste. Soy and coconut creamer is available in a number of flavors, all of which may be used for some additional flavoring if desired. In a pinch, regular soymilk or other milk alternatives can be substituted, although the end results might not be quite as rich and thick.

Soy Flour

Ah, what can't that wonder bean do? Going by the name of soya in many parts of the world, soybeans can be dried and finely ground to produce flour. Due to the fat content, soy flour contributes to the density of baked goods and has textural properties similar to those of cocoa powder, but obviously with a much different taste. There are a number of different types of flour made from soybeans, each with varying fat contents. Most of these varietals are only available for commercial use, while one type commonly appears on natural food store shelves. Don't stress, just buy the one that you can find.

Sprinkles

What's an ice cream sundae without a generous handful of sprinkles glittering on top? Though these colorful toppers are made primarily of edible wax, they are often coated in confectioner's glaze, which is code for mashed-up insects, to give them their lustrous shine. Happily, you can now find specifically vegan sprinkles (sold as Sprinkelz) produced by the Let's Do company, in both chocolate and colored versions, which can be found at just about any health food store.

Tahini

A staple for Middle Eastern cuisine, most regular grocery stores should be able to accommodate your tahini requests. Tahini is a paste very much like peanut butter, but made from sesame seeds rather than nuts. If you don't have any on hand and a trip to the market is not in your immediate plans, then any other nut butter will provide exactly the same texture within a recipe, though it will impart a different overall taste. You can also make your own just like you would make nut butter, but a high-speed blender is highly recommended to achieve a smooth texture.

Tofu

Yes, I bake with tofu and I'm not ashamed to admit it! It lends fabulous moisture, structure, and even a punch of protein to boot! When I use tofu for baked goods, I always reach for the aseptic shelf stable packs. Not only do they seem to last forever when unopened, but also they blend down into a perfectly smooth liquid when processed thoroughly, not a trace of grit or off flavors to be found. The most common brand is Mori-Nu, which is found all over the place, especially in Japanese and natural food stores, so just keep an eye peeled and you should have no problem locating it.

Turbinado Sugar

Coarse light brown granulated sugar, I just love the sparkle that this edible glitter lends when applied to the outside of cookies. Though it's not the best choice for actually baking with since the large crystals make for an uneven distribution of sweetness, it adds a satisfying crunch and eye appeal when used as decoration. Turbinado sugar is very easy to find, in any typical grocery store or megamart in the baking department.

Vanilla (Extract, Paste, and Beans)

Arguably one of the most important ingredients in a baker's arsenal, vanilla is found in countless forms and qualities. It goes without saying that artificial flavorings pale in comparison to the real thing, but plain old pure vanilla extract can usually do the trick for most applications. Madagascar vanilla is the traditional full-bodied vanilla that most people tend to appreciate in desserts, so stick with that and you can't go wrong. Happily, it's also the most common and moderately priced variety. To take your desserts up a step, vanilla paste brings in the same amount of flavor, but includes those lovely little vanilla bean flecks that makes everyone think you busted out the good stuff and used whole beans. Vanilla paste can be substituted 1:1 for vanilla extract. Like whole vanilla beans, save the paste for things where you'll really see those specks of vanilla goodness, like ice creams, custards, and frostings. Vanilla beans, the most costly but flavorful and authentic option, can be used instead of either liquid at about 1 bean per 2 teaspoons of extract or paste.

Once you've split and scraped out the insides, don't toss that vanilla pod! Get the most for your money by stashing it in a container of granulated sugar, to slowly infuse the sugar with delicious vanilla flavor. Alternately, just store the pod in a container until it dries out, and then grind it up very finely in a high-speed blender and use it to augment a good vanilla extract. The flavor won't be nearly as strong as the seeds, but it does contribute to the illusion that you've used the good stuff.

Vegan "Cream Cheese"

Amazingly, many innovative companies now make dairy-free products that will give you the most authentic cream cheese frostings imaginable. These "cheeses" also hold up beautifully in cookie dough and piecrusts, contributing a great tangy flavor and excellent structure. This ingredient is hard to replace, so I suggest that you check out your local megamart and natural food grocer, or head online if all else fails.

Vegan "Sour Cream"

Another creative alternative comes to the rescue of vegan bakers everywhere! Vegan "sour cream" provides an amazingly similar, yet dairy-free version of the original tangy spread. In a pinch, I suppose you might be able to get away with using soy yogurt instead, but that is generally much thinner so I really wouldn't recommend it. Vegan "sour cream" is sold in natural food stores and some mainstream grocers. It can often be found neatly tucked in among its dairy-based rivals, or with the other refrigerated dairy alternatives.

Wafer Cookie Crumbs

Essentially just flat crunchy cookies, available in a wide variety of shapes and flavors, there are quite a few vegan options on the market. Just be sure to check the ingredient and allergen statement, and stay away from those that look soft or chewy. For a thrifty endeavor, you could also try baking your own at home! See pages 221 and 243 for recipes. With your cookies at the ready, pulverize them into crumbs using a food processor, spice grinder, or a good old-fashioned rubber mallet, depending upon your mood. I prefer to crush mine fairly finely so that it resembles something like almond meal, but a rough crumble can lend a rustic charm too.

White Whole Wheat Flour

Move over, whole wheat pastry flour, healthy bakers everywhere have a new best friend! It may look and taste like regular white flour, but it's actually milled from a whole grain. Simply made from hard white wheat berries instead of red, the color and flavor is much lighter, making it the perfect addition to nearly every sort of baking application you can think of. I use them all but interchangeably, so if you're concerned about getting more fiber into your diet, feel free to switch out the all-purpose flour in any recipe in this book for white whole wheat.

Yogurt

Fermented by good bacteria that are said to improve your digestion, yogurt is no longer just the domain of dairy. Soy yogurts or "soygurts" are found just about everywhere these days, and you can even find some that are agave-sweetened, too. For those with soy allergies, don't despair, there are also delicious coconut yogurts available. Just double check that whatever you decide to buy is certified as vegan; just because it's non-dairy doesn't mean it's using vegan cultures. The big, multi-serving tubs are handy if you plan to do a lot of baking, but I generally prefer to purchase single-serving, 6-ounce containers for baking, to avoid leftovers that may go bad while waiting for a new application to come along. It does help to have a food scale if you decide to buy in bulk, though, so that you can weigh out the amount that would be found in one standard container.

KITCHEN TOOLS AND TOYS

Technically speaking, a mixing bowl, big wooden spoon, measuring cups, and a couple of baking tins will allow you to whip up countless fabulous desserts. Nonetheless, a few pieces of supplemental equipment will make your time in the kitchen pass much more quickly and efficiently, improve your end results, and offer the ability to produce some more adventurous recipes. Below is a quick primer on the indispensable gadgets in my kitchen:

Baking Pans/Baking Dishes

There are a wide variety of baking dishes on the market—aluminum, nonstick, glass, silicon, and so on—but any type will generally work, as long as it is the size that the recipe calls for. Just make sure to give your baking pans a little extra attention in the greasing stage if they are not nonstick. Whenever I can, I use nonstick aluminized steel, but bakeware material is greatly a matter of personal preference, so this small detail is not terribly important. For the most part, all of the baking pan shapes and sizes mentioned in this book can be easily found in any good kitchen store, supermarket, or online.

Blender

They come in all shapes and sizes, but it you want the best bang for your buck, I can't recommend the Vita-Mix highly enough. Yes, it's one of the priciest brands on the market for consumer purchase, but it's absolutely worth the investment, and will pay for itself if used correctly. There is simply no other machine that can purée nuts so completely silky smooth, or grind whole beans down to perfectly fine flour. I use mine almost every day, whether for baking adventures or just blending myself a smoothie.

Cookie Cutters

I do not use cookie cutters very often, as they can be a pain to work with. However, when necessary, I reach for big plastic ones, which are free of small details. Shapes that are too intricate tend to spread out into one big blob while cooking. Just because they make them doesn't mean they always work out well! Also, if I have the option, I stay far away from the metal cutters, as they tend to deform and rust rather easily. But, if that is all you can find, or you would rather stick with the metal, all the more power to you!

Food Processor

From whipping up the creamiest toppings to preparing homemade nut butter, food processors are one of *the* best kitchen inventions, in my opinion. For my blending and puréeing needs I use a food processor exclusively, mostly because I cannot afford a blender as well, but I also think that these machines tend to do a more thorough job of breaking down foods. Plus, they typically have a greater capacity than most blenders. Nonetheless, with the exception of grinding nuts into a paste/butter, you can substitute your blender in any recipe that calls for the use of a food processor. As long as your blender can purée, it should work fine. For large recipes, however, you may need to process things in batches if everything doesn't fit in at once.

Ice Cream Maker

One of the top kitchen toys on many foodies' wish lists, you might be surprised at how reasonably priced they run these days. All you need is a basic model that can churn at least 1–2 quarts of ice cream at a time. The most inexpensive options are those that have detachable bowls that you freeze solid before using; self-freezing units allow you to churn up much more ice cream in a fraction of the time, but start around the $150 mark and can sky rocket up to about $1000, so for the casual ice cream enthusiast, simpler is far better.

Piping/Pastry Bags and Tips

The very first time I picked up a piping bag to frost a cupcake, I knew that there was no going back. It just makes for a more professional presentation than frosting blobbed on with a knife, in my opinion. Piping bags are by no means necessary tools, but rather a baker's luxury. If you don't know how to wield a pastry bag or cannot be bothered with the hassle, there is no need to run out and buy one. However, should you wish to give piping a try, don't skimp on the quality! Piping bags come in heavy-duty, reusable fabric or plastic and disposable varieties, which range in quality. This is one time when I like to use disposable, because piping bags really are a nightmare to clean. Just avoid the cheaper plastic bags, as they are often too thin to stand up to the pressure. As for the tips, you only need one or two big star tips to make a nice "swirly" design. You can also pipe straight out of the bag for a rounded spiral.

Silpats

I simply adore these flat nonstick mats and use them at every opportunity. Likened to reusable parchment paper, Silpats cut down on the cost and excess waste of traditional single-use fibers. In terms of performance, Silpats also tend to reduce browning so that it is more difficult (but my no means impossible) to burn cookies when using them. While one should last you several years, it is helpful to have a few on hand. For best care, wash them promptly after each use with mild soap and a soft sponge. Silpats can be found at any good kitchen store.

Spice Grinder

Otherwise known as a coffee grinder, this miniature appliance is so inexpensive and efficient that every home cook should have one! Spice grinders are perfect for quickly grinding nuts, seeds, grains, and of course, spices, into a fine powder. A suitable spice grinder can be found in most supermarkets and kitchen stores.

Springform Pan

Springform pans are a must for creating perfect "cream" and "cheese" cakes. As opposed to standard cake pans, these flexible vessels boast removable sides, which allow softer cakes to remain intact when presented. Springform pans are relatively inexpensive and can be found in most food and kitchen stores, among the wide selection of baking pans. They are easily recognizable by a clamp on one side.

Stand Mixer

While hand mixers get the job done, a good stand mixer will save your arm a tremendous amount of grief. A high-quality stand mixer can cost a pretty penny, but it is usually worth its weight in gold. Powerful and independent, it is easy to multitask while this machine works its magic. If your kitchen space or budget doesn't allow for this luxury, then a hand mixer, or even the vigorous use of a whisk, will suit whenever a stand mixer is noted.

Strainer

When I call for one of these in a recipe, chances are I'm not talking about a pasta colander, with its large, spread-out holes. To sieve out raspberry seeds, drain tofu "cheese," or take care of any other liquid/solid separation jobs, a decent fine mesh sieve will never fail to tackle the job with ease. Seek out strainers with solid construction, so that the mesh won't pull out after repeated pressings with a spatula. One of about 7–9 inches in diameter should accommodate most projects, but bigger is just fine too.

TROUBLESHOOTING

Cake or bread didn't rise?

Since there are no eggs to provide leavening in vegan baking, cakes rely entirely on chemical leaveners, such as baking powder and soda. If you mismeasure these critical ingredients, there will be dire consequences, so be diligent and stick to the recipe as written! Tweaking flavors and playing around to put your own spin on things is encouraged, but altering the basic structure is not recommended.

Also, be certain to check that both baking powder and soda are in good working condition. Those little boxes tend to stick around forever, and if you don't do a whole lot of baking, chances are they've gone bad and lost their leavening ability. To test the efficacy of baking powder, place 1 teaspoon into a small dish and mix in 2 teaspoon water. For baking soda, you want to combine 1 teaspoon with 2 teaspoon of vinegar. In both cases, they should bubble up right away, or else it's time to replace them.

Yeast is a living organism (but not an animal or animal product; they're technically classified in the kingdom fungi, just like mushrooms), so it makes good sense that at some point they "die" and cease to function properly. Dried in packets, they're in a dormant state and must be reawakened before being baked. That's why most recipes recommend proofing, that is, soaking the yeast in warm water, before adding it into the dough. If after 5–10 minutes it doesn't become frothy, your yeast is a goner. I like to store my yeast in the fridge, and I've thus far never had any expire on me.

Tough, dry cake or muffin?

Sounds like a gluten problem. Gluten develops when you beat or mix a wheat-based mixture too much, making it stretchy as if you were making bread dough. Unfortunately, this is not what you want for cakes. Instead of a tender crumb, that extra gluten will give you a tight, unpleasantly chewy baked good. A side effect of having more gluten in the cake is that it will also tend to squeeze out or absorb more liquid, leaving the baked good in question with a drier interior. If you're ever unsure of how much to mix, just assume that for cakes, less is better.

Dry, hard, or crumbly cookies?

The secret to cravably soft, chewy cookies is hardly a secret at all, but common sense when it comes right down to it. Bake your cookies for less time, and allow them to sit on the hot baking sheet longer to finish cooking at a slower, gentler pace. When I pull mine out of the oven, they tend to look like they're not quite done, and perhaps even still raw in the center. It depends on the exact cookie and with practice, you'll get a better feel for when exactly to take them out, but always start by baking them for the lesser amount of time suggested in a recipe. For example, if the recipe recommends 8–12 minutes, start by baking them for only 8 and check your results. Worst comes to worst, underbaked cookies can always take a second round in the oven.

Cake or bread gooey in the center?

This is quite possibly one of the most common baking problems I hear about, which is such a shame because it's very easily prevented. It's an issue of simply not baking the item in question for long enough, even though it may look browned to perfection on the outside. Always be sure to check the interior by inserting a toothpick or wooden skewer into the center, all the way down to the bottom. This method does have its pitfalls though, should there be chocolate chips that give the false impression that your cake is still raw in the middle, so you may wish to poke in multiple places. Bear in mind that the holes will show, so unless you're covering the top with frosting, this may not be the best idea!

If you repeatedly end up with cakes that are done on the outside but raw in the center, double-check your oven temperature—it's likely that it's running hot. You can compensate by dialing a slightly lower temperature than is recommended in the recipe, or by tenting a piece of aluminum foil over your baked goods in the final minutes of baking, to ensure that the tops don't burn or become overdone.

Cake domed in the center?

Don't panic—this is a common problem with a very simple solution. The easiest way to correct a cosmetic defect like this is to wait until the cake is completely cool, and then take a long serrated knife and slice off the hump. Voila, a perfectly flat cake, and a little snack for the baker! If you're worried about crumbs or want to avoid such a situation altogether, try lowering your oven temperature by about 25 degrees. It's possible that your oven might be running a bit hotter than anticipated, causing that edible mountain to form in the first place. Double-check next time by placing an additional thermometer inside the oven, and compare the readings to the external display.

Flat muffins with no tops?

Exactly the opposite of the problem described directly above; in this case, you might want to consider raising the oven temperature 25 degrees. Additionally, make sure your batter isn't too runny; it should definitely be thicker than cupcake batter. Don't be shy when you fill the tins, because unlike cupcakes, you want to mound these up right to the top, and possibly even over. Make sure you do pile on the batter right in the center, to encourage those golden brown peaks to form.

Cupcakes remove their own papers?

Yes, nudist cupcakes. Some people never experience this phenomenon, and I hadn't until very recently when baking a large batch (16 dozen) cupcakes for a massive order at work. All was going according to plan, little cakes marching out of the oven left and right, but then while they sat on the counter cooling, they began to spontaneously undress. After having this happen a couple times on giant batches, I've come to find that there are two issues that could be the culprit here; most likely, the cupcakes are placed too close together while cooling, thus "steaming" each other and causing too much moisture to form between the cake and wrapper. Being paper, it doesn't take much for the wrapper to give up the fight and fall off.

Second, it's possible that there is too much oil in the cakes. That was my main problem, because although I scaled up the recipe, I simply multiplied most of the amounts. It's not a straight conversion when you get into such large-scale baking. I've been cutting back on the oil for batches of more than 4 dozen, and my cupcakes have stayed properly dressed ever since.

Cupcakes won't come out of their papers?

Unfortunately, the only thing that can be done about this problem is to buy different cupcake papers next time. Most manufacturers use paper that is at least somewhat waterproof, and some of the higher-quality options are even laminated or coated in food-grade silicon, like a nonstick pan, to make for easier cupcake removal. However, the cheapest options are unlikely to offer any easy-release guarantees, and if you find that your cakes keep getting trapped in their wrappers time and again, you may want to start looking into other brands.

Ice cream too hard or not creamy?

Ice cream can be a tricky dessert to make, simply because the texture is largely dependent on the machine that you use to churn it in. If the machine churns too slowly, it will cause larger ice crystals to form, thus giving you an icier finished dessert. Additionally, if it doesn't mix in much air—which is what gives the ice cream greater volume (often called "overrun" in ice cream speak)—then it can ultimately freeze much denser, which can translate into hard ice cream.

Another thing you may want to check is what temperature your freezer is. The average freezer runs at around 0°F. If yours clocks in far below that, you'll undoubtedly get more solidly frozen ice cream straight from the chill chest. Finally, bear in mind that the longer your ice cream sits in the freezer, the harder and also drier it will become. Yes, ice cream *can* go bad and become freezer burnt if you stash it for over 4 months or so, although I must admit, I've never found that to be a problem in this household.

The best solution for almost all of these problems is to simply remove your ice cream from the freezer 10–15 minutes before you want to serve it. This will allow it to soften slightly, become easier to scoop, and reach a temperature where the flavors will be more pronounced (since our taste buds can't detect flavors as well when foods are colder). If you're in a rush, you can also microwave it for bursts of 5 seconds at a time, until soft enough to scoop but not melted.

Frosting not light and fluffy?

Patience, grasshopper! Although the frosting may be smooth and creamy after just a minute of whipping, it takes much more time for it to take in enough air to become lighter in texture. Give it a solid 5–10 minutes before panicking, and if that doesn't do it, you may want to add a teaspoon or two of water if it seems too thick, or ½–1 cup more confectioner's sugar if you think it might be too thin. Make sure that you have the whisk attachment installed in your stand mixer, and crank it up to high.

Baked goods didn't turn "golden brown"?

Browning is another form of caramelization, and for caramelization to occur, you must have sugars and heat present. Since the recipes in this cookbook all have some form of sugar and of course, baked goods go into the oven, the problem probably lies in a mismeasurement, erring on the side of too little sugar. Otherwise, your sweets were simply not baked for enough time.

Chips, nuts, and berries all sank to the bottom?

All of these goodies tend to be much heavier than the batter of most cakes or bar cookies, so it's a simple matter of gravity taking over when you find them all clumped at the bottom. However, by coating the mix-ins evenly in flour before adding the wet ingredients in, you stand a fighting chance of keeping them distributed throughout. If they still fall and this bothers you, you can instead try sprinkling them on top of the batter once spread in the pan so that they may ultimately end up in the middle instead.

SPRING

AVOCADO CRÈME PIE

Makes 8–10 servings

Although this recipe may sound bizarre at first, it makes a lot more sense when you remember that avocados are actually fruits! They work just as well as, if not better than, many other fruits nestled into a sweet crust—you wouldn't think twice about a banana crème pie, right? Unlike any other mix of flavors I can think of, this is one that you'll just need to taste and experience for yourself. Since avocados are one of the first things on the market when the calendar announces that spring has arrived, this vividly colored pastry is an excellent dessert to kick off the season.

Graham Cracker Crust:
1 ½ Cups Graham Cracker Crumbs
5 Tablespoons Margarine or Coconut
    Oil, Melted

Avocado Filling:
2 Medium Avocados, Peeled and
    Pitted

1 Tablespoon Lemon Juice
½ Teaspoon Lemon Zest
½ Teaspoon Vanilla Extract
1 8-Ounce Container Vegan "Cream
    Cheese"
⅓ Cup Brown Rice Syrup
2 Tablespoons Coconut Oil, Melted
¼ Teaspoon Salt

¾ Cup Granulated Sugar
¼ Cup Plain Non-Dairy Milk
2 Tablespoons Arrowroot

Preheat your oven to 350°F and lightly grease and flour a 9-inch pie tin.

Combine the graham cracker crumbs and melted margarine thoroughly so that there are no dry patches, and pour all of it into your prepared pan. Bake for about 15 minutes, until set and lightly browned around the edges. Set aside and let cool.

Pull out your blender or food processor, and first purée the avocado with the lemon juice. Once completely smooth, add in the zest, vanilla, "cream cheese," rice syrup, coconut oil, and salt, and pulse to combine.

Place the sugar, nondairy milk, and arrowroot in a medium saucepan over the stove on moderate heat. Whisk thoroughly to break up any lumps of starch. Cook to a rolling boil, at which point the sugar should be completely dissolved and the liquid significantly thickened. Stream this syrupy mixture into your machine while it's running, and blend until the mixture is entirely homogeneous, pausing to scrape down the sides as needed. Pour the filling into your crust, and chill in the refrigerator for at least 6 hours before serving, or until firmed up enough to slice cleanly.

CARROT CAKE ICE CREAM

Makes a generous 1 quart

If there was one quintessential springtime cake, it would definitely be carrot cake. Something about those vibrant orange carrots, fluffy frosting, and gentle spices just seems to fit these warmer and brighter days perfectly. It's hard to improve on a classic like this, but by transforming it into a frozen dessert, you'll get a delightful treat that's much lighter and more refreshing than any sort of baked good.

Carrot Cake Ice Cream Base:

2 Cups 100 Percent Carrot Juice
1 13.5-Ounce Can Coconut Milk
2 Teaspoons Cornstarch
½ Cup Dark Brown Sugar, Packed
½ Cup Granulated Sugar

½ Cup Carrot Purée*
1 Teaspoon Vanilla Extract
1 ½ Teaspoons Ground Cinnamon
¾ Teaspoon Ground Ginger
Large Pinch Nutmeg
¼ Teaspoon Salt

Cream Cheese Ripple:

4 Ounces Vegan "Cream Cheese"
2 Tablespoons Maple Syrup
¼ Teaspoon Vanilla Extract

Pour your carrot juice and coconut milk into a medium saucepan, and thoroughly whisk in the cornstarch and both sugars, making sure that there are absolutely no lumps. Once smooth, turn on the heat and cook gently, stirring every now and then, until bubbles begin to break on the surface. The mixture should feel slightly thickened at this point as well. Turn off the heat and mix in the carrot purée, vanilla, spices, and salt. Let cool completely before moving into the refrigerator to chill for at least 1 hour.

While you're waiting for the base to cool, you can quickly mix up the cream cheese ripple. Simply combine all the ingredients together, stirring until smooth, and set aside.

Process the base in your ice cream maker per the manufacturer's instructions, and when it's done, scoop out half of it into the container that you plan to store it in. Pour half of the ripple over it, marbling it in with a spatula. Add in the remaining and ice cream and ripple, marbling once again, and quickly slap on a lid and move it into the freezer to solidify. Serve with a sprinkling of toasted nuts or coconut, if desired.

*Carrot purée can be purchased at the grocery store, likely packaged as baby food, or made very simply from fresh carrots. Just take 2–3 medium carrots, peel, chop them into equally-sized pieces, and place them in a microwave-safe dish with a tiny splash of water. Heat for 1–3 minutes, checking at 1-minute intervals, until fork-tender. Let the carrots cool, and then purée in a food processor or blender until smooth.

CHILLED RHUBARB TORTE

Makes 12–14 servings

For years, I never gave those overgrown red stalks of celery a second glance at the market, assuming they were just as bitter and twisted as their green cousins. While it's true that they're no treat to eat by themselves, when combined with a touch of sugar and a pinch of spice, rhubarb is more than deserving of any baker's attention. Cooked down into a cool mousse and paired with a nutty almond crust, the resulting torte is similar in texture to a cheesecake, but much lighter.

Almond-Ginger Crust:
1½ Cups Almond Meal
2 Teaspoons Ground Ginger
3 Tablespoons Canola Oil

Rhubarb Yogurt Mousse:
4 Cups Chopped Fresh Rhubarb

1¼ Cups Granulated Sugar
½ Cup Water
1 Teaspoon Freshly Grated Ginger
1 Tablespoon Lemon Juice
2 Teaspoons Agar Powder
3 Cups Plain, Unsweetened Soy or
    Coconut Yogurt

Simple Strawberry Compote:
2 Cups Fresh Strawberries, Washed,
    Hulled, and Quartered
¼ Cup Granulated Sugar
2 Tablespoons Lemon Juice
1 Teaspoon Lemon Zest
1 Teaspoon Cornstarch

Lightly grease a 9-inch round springform pan and set aside.

In a small bowl, mix together the almond meal and ginger so that both ingredients are thoroughly combined. Pour in the oil and stir well to moisten all of the almond meal. Pour the crumbs into your prepared pan and press it firmly into the bottom. Let the crust chill in the refrigerator while you prepare the torte filling.

Place the rhubarb, sugar, and water together in a large saucepan and set over medium heat. Stir occasionally and cook for about 10 minutes, until the rhubarb is so tender it pretty much falls apart. Stir in the ginger and lemon juice and sprinkle the agar over the top. Quickly and vigorously whisk it in to prevent lumps from forming and cook for 1 more minute. Work quickly or the agar will begin to set up in the pan at this point.

Transfer the cooked rhubarb into your food processor or blender and add the soy yogurt to it. Blend briefly until smooth and pour it on top of your prepared crust. Smooth down the top with a spatula and let the torte cool to room temperature before moving it into the fridge. Chill for at least 3 hours before serving so that the mousse can set and become sliceable. The warm strawberry compote pairs beautifully with the cold torte and is a snap to put together. Simply combine all of the ingredients together in a medium saucepan and cook for just 5 or 6 minutes, until the strawberries break down slightly and create a sauce. Spoon over slices as desired.

*For a tangier complement, try macerating the strawberries in 2 tablespoons each balsamic vinegar and granulated sugar instead of making the compote. You'd be surprised how a little touch of acid can really make the fresh berry flavor sing!

COCO-NUT MACAROONS

Makes 5–6 dozen small cookies

Come Passover, the most popular cookie around is the traditional coconut macaroon. As a kid, I never understood the appeal of those coarse, toothachingly sweet, and often stale balls of dusty coconut. It wasn't until I took it upon myself to rewrite the recipe with a little twist (not to mention sans egg whites) that I saw what all the fuss is about. Whether you break these treats out for Passover or any other time of the year, you know they'll be gobbled up!

⅔ Cup Crunchy Peanut Butter
⅓ Cup Plain Non-Dairy Milk
⅔ Cup Potato Starch
½ Cup Granulated Sugar
½ Cup Brown Rice Syrup

2 Teaspoons Vanilla Extract
¼ Teaspoon Salt
5 Cups Unsweetened, Shredded Coconut (about 14 Ounces)

Preheat your oven to 350°F and line two baking sheets with Silpats or parchment paper.

Grab your food processor and put in the potato starch, sugar, vanilla, and salt, and process to combine. Add in all of the coconut and pulse just a few times to incorporate it, but don't go crazy because you don't want to break it up too much.

Use a small cookie scoop of about 1½ tablespoons capacity or 2 regular spoons to drop dollops of the batter onto your prepared sheets. Bake for 10–14 minutes until golden brown on top. Coconut can quickly go from nicely browned to blackened and burnt, so keep an eye on the cookies while they're in the oven. Let cool completely on the sheets before storing in an airtight container at room temperature.

*Add an extra something special by melting about 6 ounces of dark chocolate and then dipping the bottoms of the cookies in it. Let them rest on a clean Silpat until the chocolate has set, and then store as described above.

COFFEE POPPY SEED CAKE

Makes 10–12 servings

Poppy seeds have the misfortune of only being associated with citrus when it comes to dessert. Always playing second fiddle and never in the spotlight, their potential is entirely overlooked. Pair them with a robust flavor like coffee, however, and you'll be pleasantly surprised by the result. Nutty, crunchy, and certainly unique, this is finally a cake in which poppy seeds can shine. This coffee cake is always in high demand for Mother's Day celebrations.

Crumb Topping:
½ Cup Dark Brown Sugar, Packed
½ Cup All-Purpose Flour
¼ Cup Canola Oil
1 Teaspoon Ground Cinnamon
2 Tablespoons Poppy Seeds

Coffee Cake:
6 Tablespoons Non-Dairy Margarine
¾ Cup Granulated Sugar
6 Ounces Vanilla Soy or Coconut
    Yogurt
1 Cup All-Purpose Flour
1 Cup Whole Wheat Pastry Flour
2½ Teaspoons Baking Powder
½ Teaspoon Salt
¾ Cup Plain Non-Dairy Milk
¾ Teaspoon Apple Cider Vinegar
1 Teaspoon Vanilla Extract
1 Teaspoon Instant Coffee Powder
2 Tablespoons Poppy Seeds

By preparing the topping first, it will be ready for you to quickly finish the cake and pop into the oven as soon as the batter is done. Take all of the crumb topping ingredients and combine them with a fork, until you have a clumpy mixture with crumbs about the size of peas. Set aside.

Preheat your oven to 350°F and lightly grease a 9-inch tube pan.

Using your stand mixer, cream the margarine and sugar together, scraping down the sides as needed, until thoroughly combined. Add in the soy yogurt and beat briefly. It will look chunky and somewhat curdled, but don't worry—it will smooth out once you add the remaining ingredients.

Sift both flours, baking powder, and salt together, and add them into your stand mixer. Stir for just a minute to begin incorporating the dry goods, but it still won't have enough moisture to be completely combined.

That's where the next wave of ingredients comes in: Mix the soymilk and vinegar together and let stand for 5 minutes. After that time has elapsed, add in the vanilla and coffee powder, stirring thoroughly until there are no more granules of coffee visible. Pour everything into the stand mixer while whisking on the lowest speed, pause to scrape down the sides once or twice, and continue mixing until just combined.

Spoon dollops of the batter into your prepared pan, using only half. Smooth it out so that it fills the bottom of the pan evenly and sprinkle the poppy seeds over it. Cover this layer with the remaining batter, smoothing it out again and finally topping it with the crumb mixture. Bake for 35–45 minutes, until a wooden skewer comes out of the center clean.

GRASSHOPPER LAYER CAKE

Makes 12–16 servings

Green as a leafy salad, the frosting on this cake actually gets it color from an avocado (not grasshoppers)! This dessert's peculiar name doesn't have any clear origins, but it always means that mint and chocolate was involved, and that's good enough for me.

Devil's Food Chocolate Cake:
2½ Cups Plain Non-Dairy Milk
1 Tablespoon Apple Cider Vinegar
⅔ Cup Canola Oil
1¼ Cups Granulated Sugar
1½ Teaspoons Instant Coffee Powder
3 Cups All-Purpose Flour
1 Cup Natural Cocoa Powder
2 Teaspoons Baking Powder

1 Teaspoon Baking Soda
1 Teaspoon Salt
1 Teaspoon Vanilla Extract

Crème de Menthe Frosting:
2 Medium-Sized Ripe Avocados
2 Teaspoons Lemon Juice
7–9 Cups Confectioner's Sugar
1 Cup Non-Dairy Margarine

1 Teaspoon Vanilla Extract
2 Tablespoons Crème de Menthe
½ Teaspoon Peppermint Extract

Quick Ganache Drizzle:
5 Ounces Semisweet Chocolate, Finely Chopped
¼ Cup Plain Non-Dairy Milk

Preheat your oven to 350°F and lightly grease 3 8-inch round pans, or 2 9-inch round pans.

Combine the soymilk and vinegar, allowing them about 5 minutes to curdle before use. Pour this mixture into your stand mixer and add in the oil, sugar, and instant coffee. Mix well, beating until slightly frothy. In a separate bowl, sift together the flour, cocoa, baking powder and soda, and salt. Whisk these dry ingredients briefly and add it into the stand mixer in about three additions. Give the mixer enough time to catch up with your demands before pouring in the next load, but don't let it go for too long either, or else you will overmix and end up with a tough cake. Once the dry goods have been used up, add in the vanilla and mix just long enough to incorporate. Distribute the batter between your prepared pans and use a spatula to smooth down the tops. Bake for 24–28 minutes, until a toothpick inserted into the center comes out clean. Let cool in the pans.

Meanwhile, start whipping up the frosting. Start with a very ripe avocado—this is critical, because one that is still a bit too firm will not purée smoothly. Scoop out the insides (*sans* pit) and purée in your food processor or stand mixer, adding in the lemon juice immediately and pulsing to combine. Don't worry, you won't taste this; it will just prevent the frosting from turning brown.

Toss in the margarine and turn on the motor to incorporate yet again. Scrape down the sides of the bowl as needed and make sure that it's completely homogeneous before proceeding. Slowly add in the sugar in three separate additions, making sure the top is fully covered so that it doesn't fly out, until the powder is completely mixed in and you're happy with the thickness and consistency. Add the salt, vanilla, crème de menthe, and peppermint extract. Allow the food processor to run, mixing and whipping the frosting for about 5 minutes until it's light and fluffy. Frost your cake however you like.

For further adornment, though it's really gilding the lily at this point, you can also whip up a quick ganache drizzle. Just place both the chocolate and nondairy milk in a microwave-safe dish and heat for 30–60 seconds in the microwave, until the chocolate is mostly melted. Stir thoroughly with a spatula until completely smooth, and voila, instant ganache! Drizzle to your heart's content.

HAMANTASHEN

Makes approximately 2 dozen

Asimple cookie traditionally made to celebrate Purim, it's said to be shaped like Haman's hat, and while I can't think of any good reason that you would want to eat a hat, this is one that could win the heart of even the pickiest sweet tooth. The versatile dough allows for any filling you could dream of mounding up in the center, and it's easy enough for the most reluctant of bakers to prepare. Soft and tender, these cookies are far better than the dry, sad triangles so often sold in supermarkets. And although nothing could ever beat those made by my nana, this vegan version does come pretty damn close, if I do say so myself.

¾ Cup Non-Dairy Margarine
½ Cup Granulated Sugar
3 Tablespoons Smooth Cashew Butter or Tahini
3 Tablespoons Orange Juice

1 Teaspoon Vanilla Extract
1 Teaspoons Baking Powder
2⅓ Cups All-Purpose Flour

About 1 cup jam or preserves of your choice (I just went through my fridge and used up whatever I could find—some strawberry, cherry, guava, and yellow plum preserves. Anything you like is just fine! It wouldn't hurt to throw in a few chocolate chips too.)

Using a stand or hand mixer, thoroughly cream together the margarine and sugar until smooth. Beat in the cashew butter, followed by the orange juice and vanilla extract. Mix the baking powder together with the flour, and then slowly incorporate the dry mix in until it forms a ball. It might take a bit of time, but don't be tempted to add any more liquid—it just needs a little persuasion. Cover and refrigerate for at least an hour before proceeding.

Once the dough is completely chilled, preheat your oven to 375°F and line two cookie sheets with Silpats or parchment paper.

On a lightly floured surface, roll the dough out to ¼ inch thickness. You will probably want to coat the dough itself lightly with flour, and if it becomes too finicky to roll out without sticking, toss it back into the fridge for a few minutes. Cut out circles of about 3 inches in diameter with either a cookie cutter or a drinking glass. Move the circles onto your prepared baking sheets and spoon a small mound of filling onto the center of each circle, about 1 tablespoon each. Pull up the sides of the circle in order to form a triangle and pinch the corners firmly so that they don't separate or fall down during baking. If you're really concerned about them staying in shape, you can freeze them just prior to baking, but I tossed them in the oven right away. Bake for 8–10 minutes, until lightly golden brown but still rather pale. Allow them to sit on the baking sheet for a few minutes before sliding the Silpats or parchment onto a cool surface.

ISPAHAN CRISP

Makes 4–6

Thanks to the creativity of Pierre Herme, the world has been introduced to many enchanting new flavor pairings, with the Ispahan being most famous. Comprised of raspberry, lychee, and rose water, these components are traditionally used to create a French macaron (not to be confused with a macaroon, mind you). Taking a decidedly American approach and turning it into a homely fruit crisp, this dessert is sophisticated in flavor but very approachable in preparation and presentation.

Fruit Filling:
2 Cups Fresh Raspberries
1½ Cups Fresh Lychees*, Peeled,
   Pitted, and Halved
⅔ Cup Granulated Sugar

2 Tablespoons All-Purpose Flour

Crumb Topping:
½ Cup All-Purpose Flour
¼ Cup Granulated Sugar

¾ Cup Rolled Oats
¼ Teaspoon Salt
¼ Cup Non-Dairy Margarine or
   Coconut Oil, Melted
1 Teaspoon Rose Water

Preheat your oven to 350°F.

To create fewer dirty dishes, start by simply mixing the raspberries, lychee nuts, sugar, and the flour directly in a 9-inch square baking dish.

To make the topping, you'll need to pull out a separate bowl and mix together the flour, oats, sugar, and salt. Melt the margarine and pour it in to the dry ingredients, along with the rose water. Blend until you achieve a coarse meal and sprinkle the crumbs over your fruit. Bake for 30–40 minutes until lightly browned and bubbly around the edges. Serve immediately while still warm.

*Fresh lychees can be difficult to track down, so you can also use canned lychees, as long as they're very thoroughly rinsed and dried. Seek out the cans in the ethnic section of your local grocery store, or specialized Asian markets should all else fail.

KIWI COLADA TARTLETTES

Makes about 15 tartlettes

In my neck of the woods, kiwis are just hitting their prime season around May as the temperatures begin to climb in earnest. A nice piña colada could sure hit the spot, but wait, what about those beautiful kiwis at the market? Get the best of both worlds and make kiwi colada tartlettes!

Pastry:
1 Tablespoon Flaxseeds
2 Cups All-Purpose Flour
¼ Cup Shredded, Unsweetened Coconut
⅓ Cup Granulated Sugar
1 Cup Margarine, Chilled
4–6 Tablespoons Soy Creamer

Coconut Custard:
1 Cup Coconut Milk
⅓ Cup Granulated Sugar
2½ Teaspoons Cornstarch
Pinch of Salt
½ Teaspoon Vanilla Extract
2–3 Kiwis, Peeled and Sliced

Make the coconut custard first so that it will be cooled and ready to use once the tartlette crusts are baked. In a medium saucepan, combine the coconut milk, sugar, cornstarch, and salt. Whisk thoroughly to break up any lumps before turning on the heat. Cook gently over moderate heat, stirring occasionally, until bubbles break on the surface and it feels significantly thickened. Turn off the stove and whisk in the vanilla. Cool to room temperature before placing a piece of plastic wrap on the surface of the custard and stashing in the fridge until the tartlette crusts are prepared.

Make the pastry in a food processor or by hand. For the food processor method, simply grind the flaxseed first, and then add in the flour, coconut, sugar, and margarine. Pulse until well combined and the mixture is somewhat mealy. Drizzle in the soy creamer 1 tablespoon at a time, pulsing after each addition, just until the dough is moist enough to be pressed together into a ball. To make it by hand, toss together the same mixture into a large bowl and use a pastry cutter or fork to cut the margarine into the dry ingredients. Add in the soy creamer 1 tablespoon at a time, mixing well after each addition, until you can press it together into a ball. Divide the dough in two, wrap each ball in plastic, and chill for at least an hour.

Once thoroughly chilled, preheat your oven to 375°F and lightly grease and flour about 15 3-inch mini tart pans. Turn the dough onto a lightly floured surface, sprinkle the top with additional flour to prevent it from sticking to your rolling pin, and roll it out to about ⅛ of an inch in thickness. Group half of the pans close together and lay the sheet of pastry over them all, using your hands to smooth them gently into each individual mold. Press firmly along the edges to remove the excess pastry and poke the bottom a few times with a fork so that they don't puff up in the oven. Move these pastry-lined tartlette pans into the fridge while you repeat the process with your remaining dough.

Place all of the tartlettes on one or two baking sheets for easy manipulation and bake for 14–18 minutes, until lightly browned. Let cool completely before spooning in a dollop of custard and then topping with fresh kiwi.

KUMQUAT POPPY SEED SCONES

Makes 4 scones

Tangy and sour, the bright citrus flavor of kumquats is unlike that of a standard orange, lemon, or lime. Although they have a very short season and can be difficult to find, the hunt is absolutely worth it. Should you miss the boat on this unique little fruit, you can substitute candied orange rind in this particular recipe (though it won't be quite the same).

1¼ Cup All-Purpose Flour
½ Cup Granulated Sugar
1 Teaspoon Baking Powder
1 Tablespoon Poppy Seeds

¼ Teaspoon Salt
¼ Cup Non-Dairy Margarine
½ Cup Fresh Kumquats, Chopped
2–3 Tablespoons Plain Non-Dairy Milk

Preheat your oven to 375°F and line a baking sheet with a Silpat.

In a medium bowl, mix together the flour, sugar, baking powder, poppy seeds, and salt before using a pastry cutter or two forks to cut in the margarine. You want this mixture to have some bigger and smaller lumps of margarine, but none larger than a pea. Once you get it to be the consistency of coarse crumbs, set it aside.

Chopping the kumquats into the proper size is critical to making an edible scone—too large and you'll get some rather sour bites! The way that I make sure everything is about even is I first cut my kumquats in half horizontally and remove the pips (as small as they are, they still aren't pleasant to bite down on). Then, depending on the size of the fruit, I usually will cut each half into four or six equal pieces, so they're about the size of raisins. The process of cutting up all of the kumquats can be a bit time-consuming, but trust me, it's worth the effort.

Once you've gotten through all of the fruit, drop the pieces into the flour mixture and make sure each piece is thoroughly mixed in and coated in flour. This brings in a lot of liquid, so start slow when adding the soymilk—pour in no more than a tablespoon at a time. Stir just until everything comes together into a cohesive ball of dough and pat it together into a circle with your hands. Cut this circle into four equal parts and place these triangles on your prepared baking sheet. Bake for 15–18 minutes, until nicely browned on top and a toothpick poked into the center comes out clean.

LEMON ICED TEA CHEESECAKE

Makes 12–14 servings

As the days slowly grow brighter and warmer, the need for a thirst-quenching beverage becomes all the more pressing, and not a day goes by where there isn't a full pitcher of iced tea chilling in my fridge. Though it's always cold brewed from loose-leaf tea these days, I still have a nostalgic soft spot for the instant powdered stuff infused with tart but artificial lemon flavoring. It's a fondness I learned from my dad, who always kept powdered iced tea on hand to mix up a glass at a moment's notice. He's since graduated to drinking real iced tea as well, but the powdered mix has found another role in the kitchen. That tangy citrus essence is the perfect contrast to a rich cheesecake base, and when chilled, it's quite refreshing as well.

Vanilla Crust:
1 ¼ Cups Vanilla Wafer Cookie
   Crumbs
¼ Cup Almond Meal
¼ Cup Margarine, Melted

Lemon Iced Tea Cheesecake:
1 12-Ounce Package Extra Firm
   Silken Tofu
2 8-Ounce Packages Vegan "Cream
   Cheese"
⅔ Cup Granulated Sugar

⅔ Cup Unsweetened Instant Iced Tea
   Powder
1 Tablespoon Cornstarch
1 Tablespoon Lemon Zest
3 Tablespoons Lemon Juice

Whipped Crème, to serve (p 236)

Preheat your oven to 350°F and lightly grease a 9-inch round springform pan.

Toss the vanilla cookie crumbs and almond meal into a medium bowl. Pour the melted margarine over the crumbs and stir to combine. Using your hands, press the mixture into the bottom of your prepared pan so that it's in one even layer. Bake 10 minutes and set aside.

For the filling, drain the tofu of any excess water and blend it in your food processor or blender until smooth. Add in the "cream cheese" and pulse to incorporate. Scrape down the sides and blend again, ensuring that no lumps remain before adding the sugar, iced tea powder, cornstarch, lemon zest, and juice. Purée thoroughly until completely smooth and creamy.

Pour the cheesecake filling on top of the par-baked crust and smooth out the top with your spatula. Tap it gently on the counter a few times to knock out any air bubbles and slide it into the oven. Bake for 38–42 minutes, until the edges appear set and begin pulling away from the sides of the pan ever so slightly. The center should still be a bit wobbly when tapped.

Let the cake cool completely before moving it into the refrigerator, where it will continue to firm up until it is sliceable, after a minimum of 4 hours. Top with dollops of whipped crème if desired.

LEMONGRASS MAC-NUT BLONDIES

Makes 9–12 bars

Exotic as it may sound, lemongrass is actually easy to find in most ethnic grocery stores, and even some standard markets. Lending a bright tropical flavor to anything it is infused with, it's perfect for creating a delicious blondie with a twist. Buttery macadamia nuts provide a satisfying crunch, and should you be able to get your hands on some vegan white chocolate chips, they would be a fantastic addition to these bars as well.

½ Cup Non-Dairy Margarine
½ Cup Dark Brown Sugar, Packed
½ Cup Granulated Sugar
3 Stalks Dried Lemongrass, or 1 Stalk Fresh

⅓ Cup Coconut Milk
½ Teaspoon Lemon Zest
1¼ Cup All-Purpose Flour
¼ Teaspoon Baking Powder
Pinch Salt

1 Teaspoon Vanilla Extract
1 Cup Macadamia Nuts, Divided

Preheat your oven to 325°F and lightly grease an 8 × 8 inch square pan.

In your stand mixer, cream together the margarine and both sugars so that the mixture is entirely smooth and homogeneous.

Chop up the lemongrass as finely as you possibly can—I had to use my spice grinder to get small-enough bits of dried lemongrass, so you may want to chop it into a few chunks before processing it in your spice grinder. Stir the pieces of lemongrass into the coconut milk and heat for just a minute to allow the liquid to infuse a bit. Stir in the lemon zest and let it sit for 5 minutes before proceeding.

In a separate bowl, sift together the flour, baking powder, and salt. Add these dry ingredients into your stand mixer in 2 or 3 stages, alternating with the coconut mixture, and allowing the mixer enough time to fully incorporate each addition. Mix in the vanilla and about ¾ of the nuts, and stir just until combined.

Pour the batter into your prepared pan and gently press the remaining nuts into the top. Bake for 30–40 minutes, until no longer shiny, the edges are firmly set, but it's still moist on the inside. Let cool completely before cutting.

LUSCIOUS LEMON MOUSSE

Emerging from a winter of heavy, hearty foods, when spring arrives, I typically want something light for dessert. Mousse can sometimes err on the rich, dense, and unctuous side, but not this lemony delight! Making it a perfect palate cleanser or sweet tooth satisfier, this is one dessert that you'll always be able to find room for.

½ Cup Granulated Sugar
3 Tablespoons Cornstarch
1½ Cup Plain Non-Dairy Milk
¼ Cup Lemon Juice

Zest of 1 Lemon
½ Teaspoon Vanilla Extract
1 Cup Vegan "Sour Cream," or Puréed Extra Firm Silken Tofu

In a small saucepan, combine the sugar and cornstarch, and then slowly pour in the soymilk and lemon juice while whisking vigorously. Immediately turn the heat on to medium—if you wait too long, the mixture will curdle and separate. Continue to whisk occasionally, and as soon as it comes to a full boil, the liquids should feel significantly thickened. Turn off the heat, whisk in the zest and vanilla, and let cool to room temperature. Place a piece of plastic wrap directly on top of the surface and thoroughly chill before proceeding, about 1 hour. Once completely cool, fold in the "sour cream" or tofu, and pipe or spoon the mousse into individual cups. Keep refrigerated until you're ready to serve.

MARBLED CHOCOLATE AND ZUCCHINI BREAD

Makes 10–12 servings

One of the first vegetables that becomes plentiful after the ground thaws is zucchini. Of course, they then continue to grow uninhibited all the way through summer, so zucchini overload is pretty much unavoidable. The best way to deal with this dilemma? Pull out those loaf pans and bake some bread! This bread has a rich swirl of chocolate marbled throughout. You'll never "suffer" from an overabundance of zucchinis again!

6 Tablespoons Non-Dairy Margarine
1 Cup Granulated Sugar
¼ Cup Dark Brown Sugar, Packed
1⅔ Cups All-Purpose Flour
1 Teaspoon Baking Soda
¼ Teaspoon Baking Powder

½ Teaspoon Salt
1 Teaspoon Ground Cinnamon
2 Cups Shredded Zucchini
¾ Cup Non-Dairy Milk
1 Tablespoon Apple Cider Vinegar
1 Teaspoon Vanilla Extract

¼ Cup Natural Cocoa Powder
½ Cup Mini Semisweet Chocolate
    Chips, or Finely Chopped
    Chocolate

Preheat your oven to 350°F and grease a 9 × 5–inch loaf pan.

With your stand mixer, cream the margarine and both sugars together thoroughly. Mix together the flour, baking soda and powder, salt, and cinnamon in a separate bowl. Slowly add in the dry mix, giving the mixer time to catch up and incorporate the new ingredients. Mix until mostly smooth, but don't go crazy and overdo it; a few lumps are just fine. Squeeze the shredded zucchini lightly to remove some of the excess water, and add that in along with the soymilk, vinegar, and vanilla.

Divide the batter, pouring half into a separate bowl. Add cocoa powder and chocolate chips to one half and mix so that it's smooth and homogeneous. Add alternate dollops of the plain and chocolate batter into your prepared pan until both are used up, and then run a spatula through the whole thing to lightly marble the two together.

Bake until wooden skewer inserted into center comes out clean, about 50–60 minutes. Cool in the pan for 10 minutes before turning out and moving to a wire rack.

MEXICAN CHOCOLATE CRÈME CARAMEL

Makes 6 servings

I don't pretend to be an expert on Mexican culture or traditions, but I like celebrations and I love Mexican chocolate! So one year for Cinco de Mayo I decided to experiment. The result was an incredibly decadent, sweet, and slightly spicy dessert that no chocoholic can refuse. It may take a bit of patience to assemble, but your hard work will be rewarded!

Caramel:

⅓ Cup Granulated Sugar

3 Tablespoons Water

1 Teaspoon Corn Syrup

Mexican Chocolate Crème:

6 Ounces Bittersweet Chocolate, Finely Chopped

1 12-Ounce Package Extra Firm Silken Tofu

½ Cup Granulated Sugar

1 Teaspoon Ground Cinnamon

¼ Teaspoon Ground Cayenne Pepper

¼ Teaspoon Chili Powder

Pinch Freshly Cracked Black Pepper

¼ Teaspoon Salt

½ Teaspoon Vanilla Extract

Preheat your oven to 325°F and lightly grease 6 2-ounce or 4-ounce ramekins. You'll end up with a taller crème caramel if you use the smaller ramekins, but don't be tempted to simply fill a few larger ones to the top, as this dessert is extremely rich!

Place the sugar, water, and corn syrup for the caramel in a medium saucepan over low heat. Stir just until the sugar dissolves and then stop to prevent crystallization. Increase the heat to medium high and cook until the syrup turns a deep golden brown. Quickly remove from the heat; divide the hot caramel equally among the 6 ramekins. Tilt each ramekin around so that the caramel completely covers the bottom. Let cool for at least 2 minutes.

Melt the chopped chocolate either in the microwave or in a double boiler, stirring thoroughly until smooth. Set aside, and pull out your food processor or blender. Drain any excess liquid out of the tofu, and then toss it into the machine to purée it. Scrape down the sides and add the sugar, spices, salt, and vanilla. Blend thoroughly before pouring in the melted chocolate. Pulse to combine, scraping down the sides of the bowl once more to ensure that the mixture is completely homogeneous. Pour the chocolate crème into each caramel-lined ramekin, and then place each ramekin into a large baking pan (anything but glass!).

Pour boiling water into the pan so that it reaches about halfway up the sides of the ramekins, taking care not to splash it into the custard. Bake for 45–50 minutes, until the tops are mostly set but they still jiggle a bit when tapped. Use tongs to remove the ramekins from the water bath, and let stand at room temperature for 5 minutes before inverting onto a plate.

You could also make these ahead of time and keep them refrigerated. When you're ready to serve, simply dip the ramekins into boiling water for about a minute to liquify the caramel again, run a knife around the sides to loosen it, and tip the whole thing out onto a plate.

MIMOSA TIRAMISU

Makes 6–8 servings

Instead of just drinking a mimosa with your brunch, now you can eat one too! With this play on tiramisu, orange takes the place of espresso, and champagne is used instead of coffee liqueur. A familiar assembly with a whole new lease on life, this one is guaranteed to impress. You can make a large pan of it like you usually would for tiramisu, or create parfaitlike individual servings in glasses.

2 Batches Ladyfingers (page 232)
Mimosa Syrup:
¼ Cup Orange Juice
¼ Cup Water
¼ Cup Granulated Sugar
½ Cup Champagne

Sweet Macadamia Ricotta:
½ Cup Unsalted Macadamia Nuts
1 12-Ounce Package Extra Firm
  Silken Tofu
⅓ Cup Granulated Sugar

1 Tablespoon Orange Juice
¼ Teaspoon Vanilla
Pinch Salt
Orange Zest, to Garnish

To prepare the syrup, simply combine the orange juice, water, and sugar in a small saucepan, and place over medium heat. Whisk every now and then, just until the sugar has dissolved. Turn off the heat and add in the champagne. Set aside.

For the macadamia ricotta, start by tossing the nuts into your food processor or blender, and process for 5–10 minutes, until it becomes a smooth paste. Drain any excess water away from the tofu before adding it in, and purée as well. Scrape down the sides to make sure you're not missing any lumps, and add in the sugar, orange juice, vanilla, and salt. Pulse to combine so that the mixture is smooth and homogeneous.

When you're ready to assemble the tiramisu, take your lady fingers and dip them briefly into the mimosa syrup, submerging them for no more than 2 seconds so that they don't become entirely soggy. Arrange the soaked cookies along the bottom of an 8-inch square pan, cutting them to fit if necessary. Pour half of the macadamia ricotta over the cookies, smooth into an even layer, and then add another layer of syrup-dipped cookies. Smooth the remaining ricotta over the top, and refrigerate the pan for at least 4 hours or overnight so that the flavors can meld. Top with orange zest or white chocolate curls before serving.

You can also prepare this like mini trifles, in smaller, individual dishes.

MOJITO SUGAR COOKIES

Makes about 3 dozen

Quit muddling and start mixing! Crisp, bright flavors like that of the mojito should appear in far more baked goods, if you ask me. Flecked with mint and lime zest, these sugar cookies may be simple to make but are very complex in flavor. They are delightful when served chilled.

Mojito Sugar Cookies:
1 Cup Non-Dairy Margarine
1 Cup Granulated Sugar
2 Teaspoons Lime Zest
2 Tablespoons Fresh Mint, Finely Chopped
2 Cups All-Purpose Flour
1½ Teaspoons Baking Powder
¼ Cup Plain Vegan "Sour Cream"

Rum Glaze:
1¼ Cups Confectioner's Sugar
2 Tablespoons Dark Rum
½ Teaspoon Vanilla Extract

Preheat oven to 350°F and line two baking sheets with Silpats or parchment paper.

With your stand mixer, cream together the margarine and sugar until smooth and fluffy. Add in the zest and mint, creaming once more to incorporate and evenly distribute throughout the mixture. If you were to add these in later, it would be more difficult to have the flavor spread throughout the dough without overmixing it. Slowly sift in the flour and baking powder, and then add in the "sour cream," mixing just until the dough comes together. You may have to use your hands to press it into a cohesive ball, but the key is to stop mixing when you think it's nearly done.

Pinch off pieces about the size of walnuts, roll them into balls, and then flatten them out slightly on your prepared sheets using the bottom of a glass or the palm of your hand. Place the whole sheet of unbaked cookies in the freezer for 15–20 minutes, until thoroughly chilled, to prevent them from spreading too much. Bake for 8–10 minutes, or until firm, but still pale and not quite browned around the edges.

To make the glaze, simply whisk the confectioner's sugar, rum, and vanilla together until smooth, and drizzle over the cooled cookies.

OLIVE OIL ICE CREAM

Makes 1
generous pint

Olive oil desserts are more than just a trendy gimmick—the fruity notes and richness of the olives really do suit sweet applications beautifully! In this chilly treat, you can definitely taste the delicate nuances of the olive oil, so only use the best here. A pinch of fresh herbs adds in a touch of crisp, clean flavor perfectly suited for a fresh new growing season, but a cinnamon stick or a handful of cardamom pods would make for fantastic spicy substitutions as well.

¼ Cup Loosely Packed Mint or Basil Leaves
1¼ Cups Plain Soymilk
½ Cup Granulated Sugar
¼ Teaspoon Salt

¼ Teaspoon Vanilla Extract
1 Teaspoon Lemon Juice
1 Cup Extravirgin Olive Oil

Finely chop and bruise your mint to release more flavor and add it to the soymilk. Heat briefly to scald the soymilk. (This is the point just before it comes to a boil. Never take it to a full boil, or it will bubble out of your pot and make a huge mess!) Remove from heat, cover, and let steep for 20 minutes. After that time has elapsed, strain out the mint and stir in the sugar and salt. There should be enough residual heat to dissolve both, but if not, return to the stove for just a minute or two until you can't feel any more grains in the mixture. Thoroughly chill before stirring in lemon juice and moving the whole mixture into a food processor. Run the motor while very, very slowly streaming in oil. Take your time with this one, because if you feed in too much oil at once, the emulsion will break and you'll have a separated oil slick on your hands. Finally, process everything in your ice cream machine according to the manufacturer's instructions.

Serve with cacao nibs to accentuate the fruity notes of the olive oil.

SAMOA TART

Makes 10–14 servings

Girl Scouts may be selling cookies all year round, but in my neighborhood, it was always during the first few months of spring that they started ringing our doorbells. Everyone has their favorites, but the one that I started missing the most were the coconut and chocolate delights known as "samoas," now renamed and reformulated, but still not vegan. Rather than bemoan the lackluster ingredients and pine for these cookies while everyone else indulged, I decided to one-up those conniving girl scouts and make this idea into an even better creation—a rich tart, filled with dulce de coco and topped with dark chocolate ganache. Nothing this good would ever come out of a box!

Press-in-Pan Crust:
1 Cup All-Purpose Flour
⅓ Cup Whole Wheat Pastry Flour
1 Teaspoon Granulated Sugar
Pinch Salt
¼ Cup Canola Oil
¼ Cup Plain Non-Dairy Milk
½ Teaspoon Vanilla Extract

Coconut-Caramel Filling:
1¾ Cups Unsweetened Shredded
  Coconut
1 Batch Dulce de Coco (page 223)
1 Tablespoon Plain Non-Dairy Milk
¼ Teaspoon Salt

Ganache Topping:
⅓ Cup Semisweet Chocolate Chips
1 Teaspoon Canola Oil

Preheat your oven to 350°F and lightly grease a rectangular tart pan with removable bottom.

This is one of the easiest crusts that you could make, so those that are pastry impaired need not fear. Just mix together both flours, sugar, and salt in a large bowl so that all of the ingredients are well distributed. Separately, whisk the oil, soymilk, and vanilla together, and pour these wet ingredients into the main bowl. Stir to combine, using your hands to press the mixture together if it becomes too thick to handle with a spatula. Gather the dough together in a ball, and move it into your prepared pan. Use your hands once more to press it evenly across the bottom, up the sides, and into the corners of the pan. Dock the bottom by poking it all over with the tines of a fork, and bake for 15–20 minutes until golden brown. Let cool.

To make the filling, take the dulce de coco and place it in a microwave-safe dish. Heat it for 15–30 seconds just to soften and melt it a bit, and stir in the coconut, soymilk, and salt. Once everything is incorporated, pour the mixture into your cooled crust and spread it out evenly to fill the whole tart.

For the finishing touch, melt the chocolate chips together with the oil, stirring until completely smooth, and drizzle over the top of the tart as desired.

SPRING FLING MUFFINS

Makes 12 muffins

As fresh produce suddenly returns to barren markets after the end of winter, I can hardly resist snapping up anything and everything available. Inevitably, there's always more than I can fit into my daily cooking, and I end up with a little of this and a little of that cluttering my fridge. These muffins are a great excuse to use up some leftover produce, so feel free to swap out the rhubarb or strawberries for anything from apples to frozen berries, depending on what you happen to have.

Strawberry-Rhubarb Muffins:
1 Cup Non-Dairy Milk
1 Teaspoon Apple Cider Vinegar
⅔ Cup Dark Brown Sugar, Packed
¼ Cup Canola Oil
1 Teaspoon Vanilla Extract

1½ Cups Finely Diced Fresh Rhubarb
1 Cup Chopped Fresh Strawberries
1½ Cups Whole Wheat Pastry Flour
1 Cup All-Purpose Flour
1 Teaspoon Baking Powder
½ Teaspoon Baking Soda

½ Teaspoon Ground Cardamom
½ Teaspoon Salt

Oatmeal Topping:
3 Tablespoons Rolled Oats
3 Tablespoons Turbinado Sugar

Preheat your oven to 350°F. Lightly grease 12 medium-sized muffin cups and set aside.

In a medium bowl, combine the soymilk and vinegar, and let sit for a minute to curdle. Add in the sugar, oil, and vanilla, stirring thoroughly until the mixture is homogeneous.

Separately, mix together both flours, baking powder and soda, cardamom, and salt, making sure that all the ingredients are completely incorporated. Mix in the rhubarb and strawberries, tossing to coat. By covering them with flour, you will prevent the fruits from sinking to the bottom of your muffins, so make sure you don't skip this step!

Pour the wet ingredients into the dry and stir just until combined. Distribute the batter evenly between your prepared muffin cups and top them with a sprinkle of both the oats and the turbinado sugar. Bake for 18–24 minutes, until a toothpick inserted into the center comes out clean. Let cool in the pan for 15 minutes before turning them out and cooling them completely on a wire rack.

STRAWBERRY CHARLOTTE

Makes 12–14 servings

The term "charlotte" can mean many things in the dessert world, but is generally described as a fruited custard surrounded by bread, sponge cake, or soft cookies. These can run the gamut from sloppy, homely mounds of carbs to fanciful and elegant concoctions. My version falls somewhere in the middle, being easy to make, delicious to eat, and beautiful to look at. Other berries can be substituted, but the strawberries turn the mousse such a gorgeous color and make such perfect garnishes, I've never felt compelled to change them out.

Cake Base:
2 Tablespoons Margarine, Melted
¼ Cup Soymilk
½ Teaspoon Apple Cider Vinegar
½ Teaspoon Vanilla Extract
Pinch Salt
¼ Cup Granulated Sugar
1 Cup Cake Flour
½ Teaspoon Baking Soda

Strawberry Mousse:
1 Pound Fresh Strawberries, Washed, Dried, and Hulled
1 12-Ounce Package Extra Firm Silken Tofu
½ Cup Granulated Sugar
1 Teaspoon Agar-agar Powder, or 1 Tablespoon Flakes
Pinch Salt

½ Batch Lady Fingers (page 232)
Fresh Strawberries

Preheat your oven to 325°F and lightly grease a 9-inch round springform pan.

This is a very simple cake batter, and it comes together quickly. Just whisk together the margarine, soymilk, vinegar, salt, and sugar until homogeneous, and then add in the flour and baking soda. Stir just to combine, and then pour the batter into your prepared pan. Bake for 15–25 minutes until evenly browned across the top and a toothpick inserted into the center comes out clean. Set aside and let cool completely before introducing the base to the mousse.

Once the cake is cool, prepare your mousse by tossing all of the strawberries into your food processor or blender, along with the tofu. Thoroughly purée, scraping down the sides as needed, until the mixture is completely smooth. Add in the sugar and sprinkle the agar over the top, quickly turning on the machine afterward so that it doesn't form lumps. Let it run for a minute to ensure even distribution of the agar, and finish it off with a pinch of salt. Pour the mousse into the springform pan and chill for at least 2 hours to let the mousse set.

When you're ready to serve the cake, start by cutting the lady fingers in half, since it's a fairly short cake. Remove the sides of the springform pan and press the lady fingers to the sides of the cake. Decorate the top with whole or sliced strawberries as desired.

STRAWBERRY-KIWI PIE

serves 8–10

This is not your grandmother's strawberry pie. It may look similar, and it may include the same ruby red berries, but by inviting those fuzzy kiwi fruits to the party, you'll end up with an entirely different beast.

Crust:
2½ Cups All-Purpose Flour
1 Tablespoon Granulated Sugar
1 Teaspoon Salt
1 Cup Margarine, Chilled

1 Teaspoon Apple Cider Vinegar
4 to 6 Tablespoons Ice-Cold water

Strawberry-Kiwi Filling:
3 Medium Kiwis, Peeled*

2 Cups Fresh Strawberries, Sliced
1 Tablespoon Lemon Zest
½ Cup Granulated Sugar
¼ Cup Tapioca Flour
Pinch Salt

To make the crust, combine the flour, sugar, and salt in a large bowl. Cut the margarine into small cubes and add it into the dry mix, tossing to coat. Using a pastry cutter or fork, cut the margarine into the flour until you achieve a dry, crumbly mixture with lumps about the size of peas (or pulse all of these ingredients in your food processor to speed things along). Pour in the vinegar, and add the water 1 tablespoon at a time, continuing to mix or pulse until it just comes together into a cohesive ball. Wrap the dough in plastic and chill for about 30 minutes before working with it further.

Divide the dough into two pieces, returning half to the fridge for the time being and placing the other half onto a lightly floured surface. Sprinkle additional flour over the top to prevent it from sticking, and roll it out to a thickness of about ⅛ inch, making it into a round shape at least 10–11 inches in diameter. Carefully fold it into quarters, without pressing down, and quickly move it into a lightly greased pie tin. Place the point of the folded dough in the center, and very gently unfold the sides so that it fills the pan, using your fingers to press it in evenly. Cut the excess dough away from the sides and add it into the second half sitting in the fridge. Place the whole pan in the fridge as well.

Preheat your oven to 350°F. In a large bowl, combine the kiwis, sliced strawberries, and lemon zest. Sprinkle on the sugar, tapioca flour, and salt over the top and toss to combine, thoroughly coating the fruit. Move all of the fruit filling into your prepared crust and set aside.

Roll remaining dough to ⅛ inch in thickness, cutting it into ½-inch-wide strips. Arrange it in a lattice design over the top of the pie and crimp it by pinching it to the edges. Bake at 350°F for 45–55 minutes, until the crust is golden brown and the fruit is bubbling away. Let cool completely before slicing.

*To easily peel kiwi fruits, cut off both ends with a paring knife, and starting from one of the cut sides, insert a spoon just under the skin and twist the kiwi so that the spoon goes all the way around the circumference of the fruit. Repeat the process on the other end, and the "meat" of the fruit will simply pop out.

SPICED BEET CAKE BITES

Makes 12–18

I admit that this dessert sounds for all the world like a crunchy-granola health food experiment gone wrong. Well, forget what you know about beets; once you taste this unlikely cake creation, you'll understand why I insist that everyone reconsider this humble root vegetable as a worthy dessert ingredient. If the carrot cake can win worldwide renown, why not the beet cake too? Plated with an impossibly rich beet caramel sauce, creamy salted caramel frosting, and cacao nib brittle, the contrasting flavors and textures play together so beautifully, I promise this pairing will turn anyone into a beet believer!

Spiced Beet Cake:

¼ Cup Non-Dairy Milk
½ Teaspoon Apple Cider Vinegar
½ Teaspoon Vanilla Extract
⅓ Cup Granulated Sugar
⅓ Cup Dark Brown Sugar, Packed
¼ Cup Canola Oil
¼ Cup Unsweetened Soy or Coconut Yogurt
1¼ Cups All-Purpose Flour
1 Teaspoon Ground Cinnamon
½ Teaspoon Ground Ginger
1 Teaspoon Baking Powder
¼ Teaspoon Baking Soda
½ Teaspoon Salt
1 Cup Shredded Red Beets (About 1 Medium)

Caramelized Beet Sauce:

3 Tablespoons Non-Dairy Margarine
⅓ Cup Dark Brown Sugar, Packed
1 Cup Shredded Red Beets (About 1 Medium)
¼ Teaspoon Salt
¼ Cup Unsweetened Soy or Coconut Yogurt

Cacao Nib Brittle:

½ Cup Granulated Sugar
¼ Cup Light Corn Syrup
¾ Cup Cacao Nibs
Pinch Salt

Salted Caramel Frosting:

½ Cup Non-Dairy Margarine
1 Cup Confectioner's Sugar
¼ Cup Caramel Syrup (page 220)
½ Teaspoon Vanilla Paste or Extract
¼ Teaspoon Salt

Preheat your oven to 350°F, and lightly grease an 8 × 8-inch square baking pan. In a medium-sized bowl, mix together the nondairy milk and vinegar, and let sit for about 5 minutes, until it begins to curdle. Add in the vanilla, both sugars, oil, and yogurt, and stir to combine. Set aside. Using a separate bowl for the dry ingredients, lightly whisk together the flour, spices, baking powder and soda, and salt. Toss in the shredded beats, and stir it around lightly to coat all of the shreds with flour. This will help keep the pieces more evenly distributed throughout the cake later.

Pour the mixture of wet ingredients into the bowl of dry, and use a wide spatula to gently stir the two together until you achieve a mostly smooth batter. Transfer your batter into the prepared cake pan, smooth out the top with your spatula, and tap it once or twice on the counter to bring any air bubbles to the surface. Bake for 18–24 minutes, until the top is lightly golden brown and a toothpick inserted into the center of the cake comes out clean. Let cool completely in the pan before assembling the dessert.

For the caramelized beet sauce, place the margarine and sugar in a small saucepan over medium heat and allow the margarine to melt. Cook the two together until the sugar has dissolved, and then add in the shredded beet and salt. Stirring occasionally, simmer the mixture for 5–10 minutes, until the beet has softened. Let cool for at least 15 minutes before transferring to a food processor or blender. Purée so that the sauce is perfectly smooth, with no pieces of whole beet remaining. Add the yogurt and pulse to combine. Store in an airtight container in the fridge; chill thoroughly before serving.

The cacao brittle is made just like any other nut brittle—begin by heating up the sugar and corn syrup in a small saucepan with tall sides over medium heat. Stir just to moisten all of the sugar, and then keep your spatula out of the pot until the very end! Swirl the pot occasionally instead of stirring, and cook the sugar until it reaches 300°F on a candy thermometer—right around the "hard crack" stage. Quickly remove the pot from the heat, retrieve your spatula, and stir in the cacao nibs. Transfer the hot mixture to a Silpat and spread it out to a thin, even layer, dispersing the nibs as evenly as possible. Let cool completely until solid, and then break into pieces.

Finally, the last component is the caramel frosting, which is mercifully fast and simple. In your stand mixer, beat the margarine by itself briefly to soften, to make it easier to work with. Add in the confectioner's sugar, caramel syrup, vanilla, and salt, and start the mixer on a slow speed. Once the sugar is mostly incorporated and is no longer in danger of flying out all over the kitchen, turn it up to high and whip thoroughly until light and fluffy, about 5 minutes. Pause to scrape down the sides of the bowl as needed to keep everything incorporated.

To assemble the dessert as pictured, turn out the cake onto a cutting board and slice it into 1-inch squares. A serrated knife may prove handy, or just make sure whatever knife you're using is very sharp for the cleanest cuts. Smooth a spoonful of sauce on as many plates as you'd like to serve, and place three little cake squares on top of or next to the sauce.

Transfer the frosting into a piping bag fitted with a large round tip, and pipe out dollops of frosting onto each of the squares. Finish it off with a small piece of cacao nib brittle stuck artfully into each dollop of frosting.

SWEET BASIL SHORTBREAD

*Makes 1–2
dozen cookies*

The first thing I ever have to harvest out of my own garden is always basil. Those hearty green herbs seem to thrive where so many other plants can't even set up roots, so by the time we're midway through the season, I have more basil than I know what to do with. Most applications tend to fall on the savory side, but believe it or not, these versatile leaves can make for a sweet addition to a zesty cookie. Your friends may not initially be able to put their finger on the flavor, but they'll certainly come back for another taste!

¾ Cup Non-Dairy Margarine
1 Cup All-Purpose Flour
½ Cup Cornstarch
½ Cup Confectioner's Sugar

¼ Cup Fresh Basil Leaves
1 Tablespoon Lemon Juice
1 Tablespoon Lemon Zest
Pinch Salt

Preheat your oven to 300ºF and line two baking sheets with Silpats or parchment paper.

Toss the margarine into your stand mixer and beat it by itself just to soften it a bit. Add in the flour, starting the mixer at a slow speed so that it doesn't send powder flying out. Once that has been completely incorporated, follow it with the cornstarch, and then with the sugar. Chiffonade (thinly slice) the basil and toss it in while the mix is still very powdery so that it's coated in flour and evenly distributed. Finally, add the lemon juice and zest, along with the salt, and simply process until it all comes together into a cohesive ball of dough. It may seem very dry and unlikely to stick together at all, but give it time—it could take as long as 5 minutes. You might need to remove it from the bowl near the end and knead the last dry bits in by hand.

On a lightly floured surface, sprinkle the dough with just a touch more flour, and roll it out to a thickness of about ¼ inch. If you have trouble rolling it out smoothly or find that it's too sticky to work with, let it chill in the fridge for 30 minutes or so before continuing. Cut into squares of about 1½ inches on each side; move to a prepared baking sheet. Bake for 16–20 minutes, until the edges just begin to take on some color, but you don't really want to brown these. Let the cookies cool on the sheet for 10 minutes, and then move them onto a wire rack to finish cooling.

ZESTY RHUBARB RIPPLE CAKE

Makes
12–14

Battling a surplus of rhubarb that threatened to turn moldy at any minute, I decided to make it into jam in hopes of preserving it a bit longer. Of course, I got a bit impatient and took it off the heat too soon, so the resulting "jam" was much more like a thick ice cream topping (which it could very happily be too!). The flavor was so perfect that it seemed a shame to recook it and potentially lose that, so I was at a loss, trying to figure out what to do with this extremely soft-set jam. Mulling it over, it suddenly occurred to me how wonderful it would be baked into a cake! And boy is it—flecked with orange zest and possessing a very tender crumb, the jam practically melts into this soft pillow of cake, but still holds its own to form an attractive ribbon throughout.

Rhubarb paragraphRipple:
1½ Cups Chopped Rhubarb
   (½ lb.)
1¼ Cups Granulated Sugar
3 Tablespoons Water
½ Teaspoon Vanilla Extract

Orange Cake:
1 Cup Plain Non-Dairy Milk
¼ Cup Orange Juice
⅔ Cup Granulated Sugar
½ Cup Canola Oil
¾ Teaspoon Vanilla Extract

2½ Cups All-Purpose Flour
1 Teaspoon Baking Powder
¾ Teaspoon Baking Soda
½ Teaspoon Salt

Begin by combining the rhubarb, sugar, and water in a saucepan over medium heat, and bring it up to a bare simmer. Cook for about 25 minutes, stirring occasionally, until the rhubarb pretty much falls apart. Turn off the heat, add in the vanilla, and cool to room temperature before you start to make the cake.

Preheat your oven to 350°F and lightly grease and flour a 9-inch round cake pan.

Whisk together the soymilk, orange juice, sugar, oil, and vanilla so that they're thoroughly combined. Sift in the flour, baking powder and soda, and salt all at once, using a wide spatula to fold the dry goods in with as few strokes as possible. Being careful not to overmix, stir the batter until just combined to achieve a tender crumb.

Pour half of the batter into your prepared pan, using a spatula to smooth it out into an even layer. Top that with all of the rhubarb mixture, and then spread the remaining cake batter on top of that. Swirl a knife through all of the layers to give it a somewhat marbled effect. Bake for 40–45 minutes, tenting the top with aluminum foil after 30 minutes if it seems to be getting too dark. The sides should slightly pull away from the pan and the cake will be golden brown all over when done. Cool completely in the pan before serving.

LEMON-PISTACHIO NAPOLEONS

*Makes
12–16
Napoleon
Pastries*

Impossibly light and airy considering that the pastry foundation is composed of dozens, if not hundreds, of gossamer-thin layers, the classic Napoleon is a delicious study in contrasts. Rich, silky smooth cream alternates with those shatteringly-crisp sheets, piled high in alternating stratum. Razor-sharp corners lined up in perfect rows behind French bakery cases, icing immaculately striped as if printed by a machine, much of their popularity stems from their innate beauty.

Needless to say, such extraordinary works of edible art can be almost intimidating to eat, let alone consider creating at home. However, Napoleons needn't be condemned by novice bakers; frozen puff pastry is the not-so-secret ingredient that makes stunning dessert possible in a snap. Though traditionally made with butter, many "accidentally vegan" versions now exist, so with a little careful label reading, you could be chowing down on homemade Napoleons even greater than anything store bought in no time at all. Rather than going down the same plain vanilla path, shake things up with a bright green pistachio mousse, brightened with a pop of fresh lemon zest. An ideal finish to any spring time meal, these impressive pastries needn't be confined to only special occasions anymore, especially when they come together so easily.

Puff Pastry:
2 Sheets (1 17-Ounce Package)
   Frozen Puff Pastry

Lemon-Pistachio Mousse:
1 Cup Shelled Pistachios, Soaked for
   1 - 2 Hours
1 Cup Fresh Spinach, Lightly Packed
1 8-Ounce Package (1 Cup) Vegan
   Cream Cheese
⅔ Cup Confectioner's Sugar
1 Teaspoon Vanilla
1 Teaspoon Lemon Zest
⅛ Teaspoon Salt

Striped Vanilla Glaze:
1 Cup Confectioner's Sugar
1 Teaspoon Vanilla Extract
½ - 2 Teaspoons Water
1 Tablespoon Natural Cocoa Powder

Take out your frozen puff pastry about 30 - 45 minutes before you want to bake it, and separate the sheets. Place each on a clean surface and allow them to thaw before unfolding. (If you haven't planned ahead, this would be a great time to start soaking your pistachios, too.)

Preheat your oven to 375 degrees before turning your attention to the waiting pastry. Unfold each sheet and use a rolling pin to smooth out the creases and further flatten out the sheets. They should measure approximately 10 x 14-inches.

Prick each raw pastry all over with a fork, to vent the steam as it bakes. Place a piece of parchment paper on top of the puff pastry, followed by a second, empty baking sheet right on top of that. This will weigh it down slightly to keep it even and manageable as it rises in the oven.

Bake for 30 minutes, until the pastry is golden brown all over. If it's still slightly pale in the center after removing the top baking sheet, return it to the oven for up to 5 additional minutes, uncovered. Let cool completely.

Meanwhile, prepare the mousse by first placing the spinach and pistachios into your blender or food processor. Pulse to combine and begin to break down. Add in the cream cheese, sugar, vanilla, zest, and salt, and blend again, pausing to scrape down the sides of the work bowl as needed. Puree until mostly smooth, with just a few very small pieces of pistachio remaining for texture.

Once the pastry is at room temperature, use a sharp knife or pizza cutter to slice each sheet into small rectangles, approximately 1 x 2-inches.

Move one third of the pastry rectangles over to a wire rack placed on top of a baking sheet. Mix up all the ingredients for the glaze, except for the cocoa, until smooth and lump-free. Use a large spoon to smooth the white glaze over each rectangle evenly. Working quickly so that the glaze doesn't have time to set up yet, whisk in the cocoa powder. Use a smaller spoon or piping bag to drizzle thin stripes across the short width. Then take a toothpick and run it up and down the full length to create the characteristic icing pattern. Let dry and harden.

Transfer the mousse to a piping bag fitted with a large round tip and pipe out even layers of the filling on top of one pastry rectangle. Place a second piece of pastry on top, cover with another layer of mousse, and finally finish the stack with one glazed and set pastry rectangle. Repeat with the remaining ingredients.

Prefer a more classic vanilla-filled Napoleon? Substitute cashews for the pistachios, omit the spinach and lemon zest, and blend the cream more thoroughly, until flawlessly smooth. To really bump up the flavor, consider adding the seeds of half a vanilla bean, too.

SUMMER

ANT HILL CAKE

**Serves
14–16**

As a child, it was always a rarity to order a dessert when eating out with my family. It wasn't so much a practice in frugality or restraint as it was in taste; almost always, we knew we could make the same offerings much better. Still, there was one particular treat at our local diner that captivated my sister and me—"Ants on a Hill." We continued to order it many times, even though the simple white cake with chocolate sprinkles was really far from impressive. Since then I've decided to make a new and improved version, including some chocolaty "ants" on the inside too, really boosting up the flavor and visual appeal at the same time.

Cake:
6 Tablespoons Non-Dairy Margarine
⅔ Cup Granulated Sugar
1 Cup Plain Non-Dairy Milk
1 Tablespoon Apple Cider Vinegar
2¼ Cups All-Purpose Flour
2 Teaspoons Baking Powder
½ Teaspoon Baking Soda
¼ Teaspoon Salt
1 Teaspoon Vanilla Extract
1–2 Cups Chocolate Sprinkles
    ("Jimmies")

Whipped Ganache Frosting:
6 Ounces Dark Chocolate
¼ Cup Plain Soy or Coconut
    Creamer
½ Cup Non-Dairy Margarine
1 Cup Confectioner's Sugar
Chocolate Sprinkles, to Decorate

Make sure you have one oven rack that is slightly below centered, with no other rack above it that might prevent your cooking vessel from fitting. Preheat your oven to 350°F and lightly grease a 3-quart oven-safe bowl.

Cream together the margarine and sugar thoroughly, and set aside. Whisk together the soymilk and vinegar in a separate bowl, and allow the mixture to sit and curdle for about 5 minutes. Sift together the flour, baking powder and soda, and salt into yet another bowl. Gradually add a couple spoonfuls of the dry ingredients to the margarine and sugar, mixing until combined, and then add in a splash of the liquid. Alternate the two until both are fully incorporated. Finally, add the vanilla and sprinkles.

Pour the batter into your prepared bowl and bake for 55–65 minutes, or until golden on top and a skewer inserted in the center comes out clean. Let the cake cool for 15–20 minutes before inverting it onto a wire rack.

When the cake is completely cool, make the frosting. Place the chocolate and soy creamer in a microwave-safe bowl or double boiler and melt it down into a smooth mixture. Let it sit for 5–10 minutes and then pour it into the bowl of your stand mixer. Add in the margarine and beat the two together, slowly at first, but then increase the spread once they are well combined. Turn the motor off while adding all of the confectioner's sugar, and start it back up slowly again. Gradually, turn the mixer back up to high and whip the frosting for 8–10 minutes, until fluffy and lightened in color.

Apply the frosting to your ant hill cake and decorate with additional sprinkles if desired.

APRICOT FRANGIPANE TART

Makes 12–14 servings

It's hard to beat the sweet simplicity of fresh apricots. Saving enough for cooking can be a challenge in itself, tempting as it is to eat them out of hand, but baked into an almond-infused tart, they're perhaps even better than nature intended. Serve with a scoop of vegan ice cream and I'm certain that everyone will magically find a bit of room for dessert!

Crust:
½ Cup Non-Dairy Margarine
2 Cups All-Purpose Flour
2 Tablespoons Light Agave Nectar
2–3 Tablespoons Vodka
Pinch Salt

Frangipane Filling:
3 Tablespoons Non-Dairy Margarine
½ Cup Granulated Sugar
1 Tablespoon Flaxseed
3 Tablespoons Non-Dairy Milk
1 Cup Almond Meal
2 Tablespoons All-Purpose Flour
½ Teaspoon Almond Extract
½ Teaspoon Apple Cider Vinegar
Pinch Salt
6–8 Slightly Firm but Ripe Apricots

You can make this pastry in a food processor or by hand. For those with food processors, place the flour, margarine, agave, and salt in the bowl. Pulse to combine, until there are no pieces of margarine remaining that are larger than a pea. Slowly drizzle in the vodka, 1 tablespoon at a time, until the mixture comes together in a cohesive ball. To make the crust by hand, place the flour, margarine, agave, and salt in a large bowl, and use a pastry cutter or fork to cut in the margarine, until all pieces are the size of a pea. Add in 1 tablespoon of vodka at a time, and mix just until the dough comes together.

Wrap the dough up in plastic and chill it for at least 30 minutes.

Preheat your oven to 350°F and lightly grease and flour one 9-inch round tart pan with removable bottom.

Roll the dough out on a floured surface to ⅛ inch thickness. Very gently fold the dough in half and then in quarters, without pressing down. Place in the tart pan with the folded point in the center. Unfold the dough, press it into the corners, and trim the excess from the edges. Poke the crust with a fork to prevent air bubbles, line the inside with foil, and fill it with pie weights, dry beans, or rice. Bake for 10 minutes, carefully remove the hot weights and press the crust back into place if necessary, and bake for another 10–12 minutes until nicely browned. Let cool but keep the oven on.

Meanwhile, prepare the filling by first creaming together the margarine and sugar until homogeneous. Grind the flaxseed with a coffee grinder or spice grinder and whiz it together briefly with the soymilk. Pour the flax mixture into the bowl and follow it with the almond meal, flour, almond extract, vinegar, and salt. Mix thoroughly to combine, and pour the frangipane into the crust. Halve the apricots and remove the stones, and then cut each half into four slices. Lay the slices out on top of the frangipane and press them in slightly. Crimp foil over the edges to prevent them from burning, and return the whole tart to the oven for 45–50 minutes, until the frangipane is lightly browned and set. Let cool completely before slicing and serving with ice cream or whipped cream.

BANANA SPLIT CHEESECAKE

Makes 12–16 servings

The oppressive heat of summer demands one thing and one thing only—ice cream. Better yet, a banana split with all of the toppings, piled high with whipped cream, chocolate, syrup, and cherries. Summer doesn't always start out so fiercely hot though, so until the temperatures really start to rise, such a chilly treat isn't always my first choice. Instead, creamy cheesecake that mirrors these same nostalgic flavors satisfies my cravings while there's still a bit of a nip in the air. That isn't to say that it won't help you beat the heat later in the season if you'd like; just toss the whole cake into the freezer and serve it cold like a classy ice cream cake.

Crust:
1 Cup Waffle Cone Crumbs
½ Cup Shredded, Unsweetened Coconut
½ Cup Almond Meal
2 Tablespoons Sweet White Rice Flour
6 Tablespoons Canola Oil
1 Tablespoon Brown Rice Syrup

Banana Filling:
2 8-Ounce Containers Vegan "Cream Cheese"
1 Cup Puréed Banana (about 3 medium)
⅓ Cup Granulated Sugar
⅓ Cup Maple Syrup
1 Teaspoon Vanilla Extract
Pinch Salt

Chocolate Ribbon:
4 Teaspoons Dutch-Processed Cocoa Powder
2 Tablespoons Soy Creamer

Lightly grease a 9-inch round spring form pan.

Preheat your oven to 325°F.

Use your food processor to pulse the waffle cones, coconut, almond meal, and rice flour, breaking up any large chunks so that you have fairly fine, uniform crumbs. Pour in the oil and brown rice syrup and pulse once more to combine. Dump out the whole mixture into your springform pan and use your palms to press it down firmly and evenly into the bottom. Place the crust in the freezer to firm up a bit while you prepare the filling.

Beat together the "cream cheese," banana purée, sugar, maple syrup, vanilla, and salt until completely smooth. Remove 2 tablespoons from this mixture and place it in a separate bowl, setting it aside. Pour the main batter into the springform pan, smoothing out the top with a spatula and tapping it a few times on the counter to release any air bubbles. Return to the reserved batter and mix in the cocoa and soy creamer. Drizzle it over the top of the cake in a spiral pattern and then drag a toothpick through it, starting at the center, radiating outward to the sides. If you don't want to bother with such a fancy presentation, just drizzle the chocolate batter over the top at will, Jackson Pollack-style. Bake for 40–45 minutes, until the sides of the cake are set but the center still jiggles slightly when tapped. Let cool completely, and then chill thoroughly before slicing.

BLACK VELVET CUPCAKES

*Makes 13
Cupcakes*

Possessing a sweet tooth the size of an SUV, I have a place in my heart for just about any sugary concoction, with the exception of perhaps one ill-conceived cake: red velvet. Bland, insipid, and loaded with artificial chemical colors, I've simply never understood the appeal of such a distasteful combination. Instead of trying to re-create the classic with a more natural source of color, it only made sense to incorporate some actual flavor while I was at it! Using crushed blackberries to create a deep, dark, purple and black shade along with a delightful fruity flavor, these little cakes are a much livelier version of their quiet cousins.

Black Velvet Cupcakes:
13 Ounces Blackberries, Fresh or
    Frozen
¾ Cup Granulated Sugar
⅓ Cup Canola Oil
1 Cup All-Purpose Flour
2 Tablespoons Dutch Process Cocoa
    Powder

1 Teaspoon Baking Powder
½ Teaspoon Baking Soda
¼ Teaspoon Salt
½ Teaspoon Vanilla Extract
1 Teaspoon Apple Cider Vinegar

"Cream Cheese" Frosting:
1 8-Ounce Package Vegan "Cream
    Cheese"
¼ Cup Non-Dairy Margarine
1 Cup Confectioner's Sugar
½ Teaspoon Vanilla Extract
13 Halved Pecans, to Garnish

To make the cupcakes, the first thing you want to do is thoroughly rinse and dry your berries. Toss them all into your food processor, and let the machine run until the berries are completely puréed. Press the pulp through a fine-meshed strainer to remove all of those crunchy seeds, and extract as much liquid as you possibly can. You should end up with about 1 cup of blackberry juice; if your measurement is a bit scant, add water until you reach that amount.

With seedless berry purée ready to go, you can now preheat your oven to 350°F and line 13 muffin tins with cupcake papers.

In your stand mixer or a large bowl, combine the blackberry purée, sugar, and oil. Stir vigorously to emulsify and set aside. In a separate bowl, mix together the flour, cocoa powder, baking powder and soda, and salt. Slowly sift these dry ingredients into the wet, stirring just until combined. Add in the vanilla and then vinegar last, mixing briefly and then quickly spooning out the batter into the prepared cups. Bake for 15–18 minutes, until a toothpick inserted into the center comes out clean.

Once the cupcakes have completely cooled, you can make the frosting by simply beating together the "cream cheese" and margarine until smooth, adding in the sugar and vanilla, and then whipping on high speed for a minute or two, until homogeneous, light, and creamy. Apply to cupcakes as desired and top each with one halved pecan.

BLUEBERRY-BEET PATÉS DE FRUIT

Makes about 36 squares

Surprisingly well balanced, this whimsical flavor combination is far more complex than your typical drugstore candy. Bright citrus notes beautifully accent the earthier flavor of beet, both of which sing backup to the sweet, fruity blueberries. Crunchy on the outside (thanks to a coating of granulated sugar) but still toothsome and chewy on the inside, the multitude of contrasts found in such a small bite-sized confection are positively addictive. Admittedly unusual, these were a hard sell at first, but one small square was all it took to gain the enthusiastic approval of my friends and family!

⅔ Cup Red Beet Purée*
2½ Cups Blueberries, Fresh or
   Frozen and Thawed

Zest of 1 Lemon
3 Cups Granulated Sugar
1 3-Ounce Package Liquid Pectin

1 Tablespoon Non-Dairy Margarine
   or Coconut Oil
About ½ Cup Granulated Sugar, to Coat

Place both the beet purée and blueberries in your blender or food processor, and thoroughly purée. Pause to scrape down the sides of the bowl every now and then, until the mixture is completely smooth.

Transfer the purée into a medium pot with high sides, along with the lemon zest and sugar. Though it may seem like a lot of sugar, don't forget that this is candy we're talking about, and the pectin requires a certain amount of sugar to set properly. Whatever you do, do not attempt to reduce the amount!

Stir well and bring the mixture to a boil over medium heat. While that comes up to temperature, grease a 9 × 9–inch square baking pan to prepare for the finished candy.

Add in the pectin, mix thoroughly to incorporate, and stir while the mixture boils for a full 10 minutes. Continue scraping the bottom and sides of the pot with your spatula to make sure that nothing is sticking and burning. Remove from the heat, add in the margarine, and let sit undisturbed for 2 minutes. After that time elapses, mix in the now-melted margarine and pour the liquid candy into your prepared pan. Allow that to come to room temperature before moving the pan into the fridge. Let chill until set, at least 2–3 hours, before slicing into small squares.

Toss the squares in granulated sugar and store in one layer in an airtight container at room temperature.

*The beet purée can be made in a number of ways. First and easiest would be to take a can of red beets, any size, whole or sliced, drain them off thoroughly, and then purée in your food processor until smooth. This method is certainly quick, and hassle free, but the flavor isn't the best. My typical approach is to take 1 or 2 medium-sized red beets, place them in a microwave-safe dish, and add in about ½ cup of water. Cover loosely with plastic wrap and microwave on high for about 10 minutes, until fork-tender. Keep them covered and let sit on the counter until cool enough to handle. Peel and purée.

BLUEBERRY BISCOTTI

Makes 2–3
dozen biscotti

As much as I love baking with blueberries, they can be a bit tricky to work with. Such fragile little berries can't stand up to aggressive mixing, folding, and beating, *especially* when previously frozen and then defrosted in the off-season. That's why this is one cookie that skips the drama of delicate mixing, shaping, and then disappointment after they still burst in the oven, by simply blending up those berries in the first place. By evenly distributing that blueberry goodness throughout the cookie, you get much more of that elusive fresh berry flavor too!

2 Cups All-Purpose Flour
1½ Teaspoons Baking Powder
¼ Teaspoon Salt
⅔ Cup Granulated Sugar

½ Cup White Chocolate Chips or
   Chopped Macadamia Nuts
2 Cups Fresh or Frozen and Thawed
   Blueberries

2 Tablespoons Canola Oil
1 Teaspoon Lemon Zest
1 Teaspoon Vanilla Extract

Preheat your oven to 325°F and line a baking sheet with parchment paper or a Silpat.

In a medium bowl, stir together the flour, baking powder, salt, and sugar, just to combine. Mix in the white chocolate or macadamia nuts so that they're distributed throughout the dry goods and lightly coated in flour. Set aside.

Toss the blueberries into your food processor or blender, and thoroughly purée. Add in the oil, zest, and vanilla; scrape down the sides of the bowl to make sure everything is being blended; and pulse to combine. Once smooth, pour the blueberry mixture into the bowl of dry ingredients and stir with a wide spatula just to bring the batter together but not overwork the dough.

The resulting mixture may seem very wet for biscotti batter, but bear with me here. Spoon it into two equal logs onto your prepared baking sheet, each about 2 inches wide by 8 or 9 inches long. The exact measurements aren't important, so don't break out a ruler or anything, but make sure that the logs are rather skinny and long, and not mounded up higher than an inch or so. Use well-moistened hands to further shape the logs if they're drastically misshapen or improperly sized, but bear in mind that you can't do extensive sculpting here.

Bake for 45–55 minutes, until lightly golden brown on top. Keep the oven on but let the biscotti loaves cool for at least 15 minutes.

Cut the loaves into ½- to ¾-inch-thick slices and lay them with one cut side down on a fresh piece of parchment or a cleaned Silpat. Return them to the oven and bake for another 10–15 minutes, until lightly browned. Flip the biscotti over onto the other cut side and repeat. Let cool completely before removing them from the baking sheet.

CHERRIES JUBILEE BUNDT CAKE

Serves 16–18

As one of the few old-school flaming desserts still available on some traditional menus, a typical order of cherries jubilee will definitely turn heads. Though nothing more than cherries, liqueur, and maybe a scoop of vanilla ice cream, it's stood the test of time and remains a nostalgic favorite, even for those who missed its heyday. My interpretation, which takes those basic flavors and combines them into a towering bundt cake, isn't nearly as flamboyant, but of course much safer for home preparation, and just as showstopping when presented to a crowd.

3½ Cups All-Purpose Flour
1¼ Cups Granulated Sugar
2 Teaspoon Baking Powder
1 Teaspoon Baking Soda
¾ Teaspoon Salt
1 Tablespoon Flaxseeds, Ground

1 Cup Fresh Pitted and Chopped
   Cherries
1 Cup Dried Unsweetened Cherries
1 Cup Unsweetened 100 Percent
   Cherry Juice
½ Cup Plain Non-Dairy Milk

½ Cup Canola Oil
1 Tablespoon Orange Zest
⅓ Cup Kirsch, Cognac, Brandy, or
   Rum

Preheat your oven to 350°F and lightly grease and flour a 12-cup-capacity bundt pan.

In a large bowl, whisk together the flour, sugar, baking powder and soda, salt, and ground flaxseeds. Once all of the dry ingredients are well distributed throughout, add in both the fresh and dried cherries, and toss to coat with the flour. Set aside.

Separately, stir together the cherry juice, nondairy milk, oil, and zest. Pour this wet mixture into the bowl of dry, and using a wide spatula, gently combine the two in as few strokes as possible. It's okay to leave a few lumps in the batter, but be sure not to overmix.

Transfer the batter to your prepared bundt pan in spoonfuls, evenly distributing it within the pan. Smooth out the top with your spatula, and gently tap the whole pan on the counter a few times to release any air bubbles that might be trapped between the batter and the sides of the pan. Side it into the oven and bake for 50–60 minutes, until golden brown on top and a cake skewer inserted into the center of the cake comes out clean.

Let cool completely in the pan before turning out onto a serving plate. Brush the liqueur all over the exterior and let it sit and soak it in for at least 6 hours. It gets even better if you allow it to sit overnight, but it may be hard to wait!

CHERRY MACAROON TART

Serves 10–12

Encased in a crust of tender coconut flakes, fresh cherries really get a chance to shine while still playing beautifully with other flavors. Cohesive enough to slice but still delectably gooey and perhaps even messy, this tart is actually much like a deep dish pie. Served warm with a scoop of ice cream on the side, this is the sort of dessert that summer fruits dream about becoming.

Coconut Macaroon Crust:
3 Cups Sweetened, Shredded
   Coconut
¼ Cup Cornstarch
¼ Cup Non-Dairy Margarine or
   Coconut Oil, Melted

Cherry Filling:
2 Pounds Pitted Sweet Cherries,
   Fresh or Frozen
1 Cup Granulated Sugar
6 Tablespoons Cornstarch
¼ Teaspoon Salt

2 Tablespoons Non-Dairy Margarine
   or Coconut Oil
¼ Teaspoon Almond Extract

Preheat your oven to 325°F and lightly grease a 9-inch round tart pan with removable bottom, or springform pan.

To make the coconut crust, break out your food processor and toss in the coconut. Sprinkle on the cornstarch and drizzle the melted margarine over. Pulse to combine and break the coconut down into smaller pieces, but you don't want to completely purée it. Once the mixture is crumbly but mostly cohesive, dump it out into your tart pan and use your fingers to press it evenly up the sides and along the bottom. Bake for just 10–15 minutes until golden brown around the edges. Let cool, and you can turn off the oven now because the filling is made entirely on the stove top.

Set a medium saucepan over moderate heat and toss together the cherries, sugar, cornstarch, and salt. Stirring occasionally, stir the mixture until the sugar has dissolved and the liquid begins to thicken, about 5–15 minutes or so—it will take longer for frozen cherries to defrost and begin to cook, so be patient. Turn off the heat, toss in the margarine and almond extract, and stir until the residual heat melts the margarine completely. Let cool for another 5 minutes or so before pouring it into your crust. Cool to room temperature and then refrigerate for at least an hour before serving so that the filling has time to set.

CHERRY-BERRY PEANUT BUTTER COBBLER

Serves 4–5

Child or adult, who doesn't love the combination of peanut butter and jelly? It's estimated that the average American eats more than 1,500 PB&J sandwiches before graduating from high school, and I can only imagine how many more there are to come in the following years. Taking a more sophisticated approach to this classic duo, whole fruits are combined to form a sweet yet balanced base for peanut-butter-enriched cobbler dough to rest upon. Forget about the white bread and unctuous jelly; this cobbler elevates the PB&J to a whole new level.

Fruit Filling:
3 Cups Sweet Dark Cherries, Pitted
2 Cups Blueberries
⅓ Cup Granulated Sugar
4 Teaspoons Cornstarch

Peanut Butter Topping:
¾ Cup All-Purpose Flour
1 Tablespoon Granulated Sugar
¼ Teaspoon Baking Powder
Pinch Salt

2 Tablespoons Crunchy Peanut
 Butter
1 Tablespoon Non-Dairy Margarine
2–4 Tablespoons Cold Water

Preheat your oven to 400°F and make sure that the racks in your oven are centered.

Combine all of the ingredients for the filling together in a medium saucepan and gently heat, just until the sugar dissolves and the berries begin to release their juices. This should take only 5–10 minutes over medium heat. Spoon the fruit into an 8-inch round cake pan and set aside.

For the topping, sift together the flour, sugar, baking powder, and salt into your food processor or a large bowl. If using a food processor, drop in the margarine and peanut butter and pulse a few times until you get coarse crumbs, much like you would want for a piecrust. Slowly pulse in the water, 1 tablespoon at a time, until the dough comes together into a ball. If you choose to do this step by hand, simply use a pastry cutter or two forks to achieve the same effect. Dump your dough out onto a lightly floured surface, either roll or pat out to about 1 cm thick, and cut into rounds using a biscuit cutter. Drop the biscuits over the top of your cobbler so that none overlap before moving the whole thing into the oven.

Bake for 25–30 minutes, until the topping is golden brown and the fruit is bubbling up around the edges. Let sit for at least 10 minutes before serving so you don't burn your mouth!

MANGO LASSI POPSICLES

Makes between 5–10, depending on the size and shape of your molds

Usually a refreshing drink made out of (what else?) mangoes and yogurt, it only takes a little bit more patience to turn this fantastic mixture into a frozen treat. The wait is more than worth it, because it's better for beating the intense summer heat, not to mention that it's so much more fun to eat food on a stick! A pinch of cardamom adds an extra little zing, and is completely mandatory in my opinion, but you could also opt to substitute ground ginger if you prefer.

2 Ripe Mangos
1 Cup Plain or Vanilla Soy or Coconut Yogurt
¼ Cup Granulated Sugar

½ Teaspoon Ground Cardamom
½ Teaspoon Vanilla Extract

These popsicles are so easy to make they barely need instructions. All you need to do is remove the skin and pits from your mangos, chop them into pieces, and purée them thoroughly in a blender or food processor. Add in the soy yogurt, sugar (you may need more or less depending on the sweetness of your fruit, so be sure to taste it!), cardamom, and vanilla. Once thoroughly combined, pour the mixture into popsicle molds and place on a level shelf in your freezer. Let freeze for about an hour before inserting popsicle sticks, so that they're firm enough to hold the sticks up straight. Continue to freeze for at least 3 more hours before serving, until completely solid.

MANGO TANGO CUPCAKES

Makes 14 Cupcakes

Like a lively dance, mangoes, macadamia nuts, and a good dose of rum are spun together to create their own harmony of flavors. Right at home at any summertime party, they're perfect single servings of tropical delight, and a whole lot of fun.

Mango Cupcakes:
2 Ripe Mangoes, Peeled and Pitted
1 Teaspoon Apple Cider Vinegar
1 Teaspoon Almond Extract
1 Cup Granulated Sugar
½ Cup Canola Oil
1½ Cups All-Purpose Flour

1 Teaspoon Baking Powder
1 Teaspoon Baking Soda
1 Teaspoon Ground Ginger
½ Teaspoon Salt
⅔ Cup Macadamia Nuts, Chopped

Rum Frosting:
3 Tablespoons Margarine
½ Cup Vegan "Cream Cheese"
4 Cups Confectioner's Sugar
¼ Cup Rum*
½ Teaspoon Ground Ginger

Preheat your oven to 350°F and line 14 muffin tins with cupcake liners.

Using your food processor or blender, purée the mangos so that you have a completely smooth mixture, equal to about 1 ⅓ cups. If your measurement is a bit scant, add unsweetened applesauce until it is equal.

Pour the purée into a large bowl, along with the vinegar, almond extract, oil, and sugar, whisking to combine. Add in the remaining ingredients all at once, making sure that the macadamias are at least mostly coated in the flour to prevent them from sinking to the bottom of the cupcakes. Fold the dry ingredients in gently but quickly with a wide spatula, stirring just enough to bring the mixture together. A few lumps are better than an overmixed and tough batter!

Divide the batter between your prepared cupcake tins and bake for 16–20 minutes, until lightly browned and a toothpick inserted into the center comes out clean. Let cool completely on a wire rack before frosting.

For the frosting, simply whip together all of the ingredients in your stand mixer, starting at a slow speed so as not to send sugar flying out of the bowl. Once mostly incorporated, dial up the speed and beat for about 5 minutes, until light and fluffy.

*Alternately, you could use a scant ¼ cup of water and 1 teaspoon rum extract if you don't want to use alcohol here.

MEAN, GREEN PISTACHIO ICE CREAM

*Makes 1
scant quart*

I like colorful food as much as the next person, but far too many pistachio ice creams out there take on an enticing shade of green through chemical means, leading to a terribly disappointing taste and a belly full of chemicals. A good version of this classic flavor doesn't necessarily need to be an emerald or forest green to be delicious, but you can still achieve such a luscious hue simply by using the nuts themselves, plus a healthy dose of vibrant green avocado for creaminess. After you taste how incredibly flavorful this easy nutty treat can be, you will find it close to impossible to justify the purchase of those fakers again.

1 Cup Shelled and Toasted Pistachios
   (or ¾ Cup Pistachio Butter)
1 12-Ounce Package Extra Firm
   Silken Tofu

1 Small Ripe Avocado
1 Teaspoon Lemon Juice
1½ Cups Plain Non-Dairy Milk
½ Cup Light Agave Nectar

1 Teaspoon Vanilla Extract
¼ Teaspoon Salt
½ Cup Roughly Chopped Toasted
   Pistachios

First things first, toss the nuts into your food processor and grind them down into a thick, doughy sort of paste. This can take as long as 10 minutes, so be patient and don't rush this step, unless you'd rather settle for gritty ice cream. Once the nuts seem to have surrendered their natural oils and are pretty well pulverized, stop the machine and drain any excess liquid away from your tofu before tossing it into the mix as well. Give it a nice long blend, being sure to stop and scrape down the sides periodically until you have a completely smooth mixture. Follow that with the avocado, lemon juice, nondairy milk, agave, vanilla, and salt, blending until everything is fully incorporated. Pour the mixture into your ice cream maker and freeze according to the manufacturer's instructions. In the last 5 minutes of freezing, toss in the chopped pistachios.

PARADISE SUNSET PARFAITS

Makes 6–10 parfaits

Layers of brilliantly colored fruits, fading into the horizon of your glasses like a beautiful sunset, these parfaits will bring a bit of the tropics into your kitchen. Despite the multitude of components, each one is very simple to make, and a breeze to assemble. If you're making them for a crowd, the parfaits can be assembled beforehand and kept in the refrigerator for up to a day. Who says you need to go on vacation to see an exotic sunset like this?

Caramelized Pineapple:
1 Tablespoon Non-Dairy Margarine
   or Coconut Oil
⅓ Cup Brown Sugar
2 Cups Cubed Pineapple Flesh

Mango Mousse:
2 Ripe Mangoes

1 12-Ounce Package Extra Firm
   Silken Tofu
½ Teaspoon Lemon Juice
½ Cup Confectioner's Sugar
Pinch Salt

Macerated Raspberries:
1 Cup Fresh Raspberries

1 Tablespoon Limoncello or Grand
   Marnier

To Serve:
1 6-Ounce Container Vanilla Soy
   Yogurt, or ¾ Cup Whipped
   Crème (page 245)

Starting with the base of caramelized pineapple, set a medium skillet over moderate heat, and melt the margarine or warm up the oil. Stir in the brown sugar and heat it until dissolved. Toss in the cubes of pineapple and stir continuously but gently to coat. Continue to cook for another 5–10 minutes until there's no excess liquid remaining at the bottom of the pan. Remove the pineapple onto a plate and let cool.

As for the mango mousse, simply remove the skin and pit, and toss the flesh into your food processor or blender. Drain the tofu of as much water as possible and add that in as well. Thoroughly purée until the mixture is entirely smooth and add in the lemon juice, sugar, and salt. Pulse to combine and set aside.

For the macerated raspberries, just combine the berries and limoncello in a small dish and lightly mash with a fork. Let sit for at least 10 minutes.

To assemble the parfaits, start by spooning a few cubes of the pineapple into the bottom of a champagne glass. Spoon a dollop of mango mousse on top and smooth it out as best as possible. Add a spoonful of raspberries, and finally, top with a thin layer of soy yogurt for contrast. Repeat in as many glasses as needed to use all of the components.

PEACHES AND CRÈME BREAKFAST BUNS

Makes about 8–10 buns

Juicy, ripe peaches smeared with creamy soy yogurt, all wrapped up in a modestly sweetened tender dough—these buns are what those sugar-coma icing bomb called cinnamon rolls at the mall can only dream of tasting like. Revitalized with bites of fresh fruit, these aren't nearly as heavy as many more decadent rolled pastries can be, making them fantastic for a special breakfast. Since the dough takes some time to rise, you can prepare the dough the night before and let it rest in the fridge overnight. The smell of these sweet, fruited buns baking in the oven will send everyone in the house racing to jump out of bed and start the day!

Dough:
½ Cup Plain Non-Dairy Milk
1 Teaspoon Active Dry Yeast
3 Tablespoons Canola Oil or
    Margarine, Melted
¼ Cup Granulated Sugar
3 Ounces Plain Soy or
    Coconut Yogurt
½ Teaspoon Salt
¼ Teaspoon Almond Extract
¼ Teaspoon Baking Powder
2¼–2½ Cups All-Purpose
    Flour

Peaches and Cream Filling:
3 Firm but Ripe Peaches,
    Chopped (about 2½ Cups)

¼ Cup Granulated Sugar
1 Tablespoon Cornstarch
¼ Cup Fresh Lemon Juice
½ Teaspoon Vanilla Extract
⅓ Cup Vegan "Cream Cheese"

Simple Cinnamon Icing:
1½ Cups Confectioner's Sugar
¼ Teaspoon Ground
    Cinnamon
Pinch Salt
½ Teaspoon Vanilla Extract
1–3 Tablespoons Non-Dairy
    Milk

Heat your soymilk for a minute or two in the microwave over the stove, just to take the chill off. Sprinkle the yeast over and let it sit until it becomes reactivated and bubbly, about 5 minutes. Pour the yeast mixture into the bowl of your stand mixer and add in the oil or margarine, sugar, yogurt, salt, and almond extract. Mix thoroughly to combine, and then add in 2 cups of the flour, along with the baking powder. Although yeast is the primary leavener in this baked good, the baking powder will serve to keep the dough a bit lighter, if not cause it to fully rise. Let the mixer slowly work the flour in, and then add between ¼ and ½ more cup of flour, depending on how wet or sticky your dough feels.

Once it has formed into a cohesive ball that is slightly tacky to the touch, use the hook attachment to knead the dough for about 10 minutes. You can also do this by hand on a floured surface, and it will take 15 minutes. When the dough is smooth and elastic, drop it into a greased bowl and cover with plastic wrap. Let sit in a warm spot until doubled in bulk, about 1½ hours.

While you're waiting, you can prepare the filling. Set a medium saucepan on the stove over medium heat and toss together the chopped peaches, sugar, and cornstarch. Add in the lemon juice and mix to combine. Stirring occasionally, cook the fruit until it has softened a bit and all of the excess liquid has thickened. Incorporate the vanilla after turning off the heat and let cool completely before using.

Lightly grease an 8-inch or 9-inch round cake pan. The size isn't so critical for these, as long as they can hold the rolls close together. Alternately, if you wanted them all to be perfectly round and separate, you could bake your buns in lightly greased jumbo muffin tins.

Punch down the dough, turn it out onto a well-floured surface, and form it into a rectangle about 15 inches long and 12 inches wide. Spread the cream cheese mixture over the dough, leaving one of the long sides clean so that you can seal the roll. Spread your cooked peach mixture over the dough next, smoothing it out so that the chunks of fruit are as evenly distributed as possible. Starting with the long side that is completely covered, roll the dough up into a tight log and let it rest on the counter with the seal side down. Use a piece of unflavored dental floss to cut slices while keeping the shape of the rolls, or use a very sharp knife and reshape the pieces as necessary. Place them in your prepared pans so that they're close but not crowded, and let them rest for another hour until they rise again and fill the space well.

As they near the end of their rising time, preheat your oven to 350°F. When the rolls are ready for the oven, bake for 26–34 minutes, until golden brown all over. Let cool in the pans and eat warm as is, or let them cool completely before applying a quick drizzle of icing.

To make the icing, simply whisk all of the ingredients together in a medium-sized bowl, adding in nondairy milk 1 tablespoon at a time, until it's smooth and reaches the consistency you'd prefer. Apply liberally to each bun.

POACHED APRICOTS

Serves 4

Summer's innumerable fresh fruits are all so perfectly delicious it's almost a shame to cook or further manipulate them. Explosively juicy and packed with flavor, apricots always tempt me away from the oven and back into the fridge, demanding to be eaten immediately as is. Still, a whole flat of these stone fruits can only last so long, and plain apricots are exciting for a week or two at most. The best way to deal with this "problem" is to poach them very simply, infusing the essence of vanilla and perhaps a bright lemony bite. If you don't have limoncello or prefer not to use alcohol, simply use an equal amount of lemon juice with an additional 2 tablespoons of sugar.

1 Cup Water
⅓ Cup Limoncello
¼ Cup Granulated Sugar

1 Small Vanilla Bean
4 Slightly Underripe (Firm)
   Apricots

In a medium saucepan, combine the water, limoncello, and sugar. Slice the vanilla bean down the center and use the side of your knife to scrape out the seeds. Place both the seeds and spent pods in with the liquids and bring everything to a boil.

Slice your apricots in half and remove the pits. Once the water has come to a boil, move the apricot halves into the pot and reduce the heat to a bare simmer. Cover and cook for just 5–10 minutes until fork-tender. They're a small soft fruit to begin with, so they don't need very much time to cook. Using a slotted spoon, remove them from the pot and let them cool for a few minutes.

Continue to cook the remaining liquid at medium heat until it has reduced to about ½ cup, and spoon it over the apricots to serve.

RASPBERRY CHEESECAKE POPSICLES

6–12 Popsicles

These popsicles are as close to instant gratification as you can get when making either a cheesecake or a frozen dessert. No baking, no churning, and before you know it, you have a whole tray of fruity, cheesy, and creamy freezer pops. Of course, any other sort of jam could be substituted depending on what you prefer or have on hand, but raspberry is my personal favorite topper for plain cheesecake, so I simply couldn't resist the combo.

1 8-Ounce Package Vegan Cream "Cheese"
½ Cup Confectioner's Sugar
½ Cup Plain Non-Dairy Milk
1 Tablespoon Vanilla Extract
1 Cup Raspberry Preserves

Simply toss the cream "cheese" into your stand mixer along with the sugar and beat the two together. Add in the soymilk and vanilla extract and mix until everything is completely homogeneous. Take out your raspberry preserves, and if it doesn't pour easily, microwave it for a few seconds just to loosen it up. Pour the preserves into the bowl and fold them in by hand with a large spatula—you can either completely blend it in or leave it slightly unmixed for a marbled or spotted effect. Pour the mixture into popsicle molds, add sticks, and freeze for at least 4 hours, until completely set and solidified.

RASPBERRY LAVENDER CUPCAKES

Makes 12 cupcakes

I must admit to being generally biased against cooking with flowers. Even when purchasing soap or lotion, I much prefer food scents to floral. However, after a bit of reluctant experimentation, it turned out that a small pinch of lavender really does go well with light fruity flavors. Rounded out by a fresh lemon icing, these cupcakes are proof that flowers truly do have their place in the culinary world.

Cupcakes:
1 Cup Non-Dairy Milk
1 Tablespoon Lemon Juice
⅔ Cup Sugar
¼ Cup Olive Oil
1 Cup All-Purpose Flour
½ Cup Whole Wheat Pastry Flour

1 Teaspoon Baking Powder
½ Teaspoon Baking Soda
¼ Teaspoon Salt
1 Tablespoon Dried Culinary
   Lavender
1 Teaspoon Vanilla Extract
1 Cup Raspberries

Lemon Glaze:
2 Tablespoons Lemon Juice
1 Tablespoon Light Corn Syrup
Zest of ½ Lemon
2 Cups Confectioner's Sugar

Preheat your oven to 350°F and line 12 standard muffin cups with papers.

Whisk together the soymilk and lemon juice and let sit for about 5 minutes to curdle. Once that time has elapsed, add in the sugar and oil, whisking briefly to combine. Set aside.

In a medium bowl, sift together both flours, baking soda and powder, and salt. Add in the lavender and raspberries and toss gently to coat with the dry mixture. Pour in the wet ingredients along with the vanilla, stirring very gently with a wide spatula so as not to break up the berries.

Drop dollops of the batter into the prepared cups, distributing it evenly between them. Bake for 18–24 minutes, until a toothpick inserted into the center comes out clean. Let rest for 10 minutes after they come out of the oven, and then turn the cupcakes out of their pans and let cool completely on a wire rack before glazing.

To make the glaze, combine the lemon juice and corn syrup in a microwave-safe dish and heat for just a minute or two until the mixture comes to a boil. Whisk in the zest and confectioner's sugar, a cup at a time, stirring until it is completely smooth. Pour a small amount over each cupcake and tilt the cupcake around in the air to achieve an even covering. Top with additional raspberries if desired and let sit at room temperature for about an hour to fully dry.

RASPBERRY MOCHA SEMIFREDDO

Serves 8–10

Every year, my dad and I look forward to nothing more than raspberry season. As soon as the first red rubies appear on the bushes near our home, we go out in full force, spending hours tramping through the woods, struggling through the thorns and vines, and amass as many of those precious berries as we can possibly carry. This is serious business—we usually get at least 20 quarts by the end of the season! As you might expect, this inspires a lot of raspberry treats. I like to switch things up and make different desserts every time, since there are so many berries at my disposal, but this semifreddo is so good I'm willing to break my own rules and make it many times over. Quicker and easier than ice cream because it's "semifrozen," you don't need any fancy equipment to make it, either!

2 12-Ounce Boxes Extra Firm Silken Tofu
1 Cup Confectioner's Sugar
1 Teaspoon Vanilla Extract

¼ Cup Coconut Milk
8 Ounces Semisweet Chocolate, Chopped
1 Tablespoon Canola Oil

⅓ Cup Coffee Liqueur
Pinch Salt
2 Cups Raspberries, Divided

Pull out either your blender or your food processor and toss in both boxes of tofu. Purée thoroughly, scraping down the sides as needed to make sure that no chunks remain. Once completely smooth, add the sugar and vanilla.

In a microwave-safe container, heat the coconut milk for just about 1 minute to warm it through. Add in the chopped chocolate and oil, and let it sit for a few minutes so that it can begin to melt. Stir the mixture to help the chocolate melt and continue to microwave in short bursts of 15–30 seconds, mixing thoroughly after each heating to prevent it from burning. When the chocolate is entirely melted and there are no more lumps, add this mixture into your tofu purée and pulse to combine. Incorporate the coffee liqueur and salt in the same way. Scrape down the sides again to make sure you have a homogeneous mixture.

Set aside ½ cup of the raspberries for later. Fold in the remaining 1½ cups of berries, being careful not to crush them while still distributing them evenly. Pour everything into 8" × 4.5" flexible silicon loaf pan, or a standard loaf pan lined with plastic wrap. Place the pan on a flat surface in your freezer and let sit for at least 6 hours until solid. If you let it freeze for longer than that, you may want to allow it 10–15 minutes to thaw at room temperature before slicing and serving. Top with the extra berries.

RED, WHITE, AND BLUE LAYER CAKE

Makes 12–14 servings

The Fourth of July demands something more patriotic than the standard dessert, but also something that will feed a crowd and stand up well for a picnic. A bit more restrained than an all-out flag cake, but still bearing the appropriate color scheme, this cake is both beautiful to serve and a delight to eat. Colored with nothing but fresh fruits, each layer is absolutely bursting with berries.

Raspberry Cake:
1 12-Ounce Bag Frozen Raspberries, Thawed
½ Cup Plain Non-Dairy Milk
2 Teaspoons Apple Cider Vinegar
½ Cup Non-Dairy Margarine
1⅓ Cups Granulated Sugar

2¾ Cups All-Purpose Flour
2 Teaspoons Baking Powder
1 Teaspoon Baking Soda
½ Teaspoon Salt
½ Teaspoon Vanilla Extract

Cooked Vanilla Frosting:
¼ Cup Cornstarch
1 Cup Plain Non-Dairy Milk
1 Cup Non-Dairy Margarine
1 Cup Granulated Sugar
2 Teaspoons Vanilla Extract
1 Pint Fresh Blueberries, to Decorate

Preheat your oven to 350°F and lightly grease and flour 2 8-inch round pans.

First things first, toss the raspberries into your blender or food processor, and thoroughly purée. Use a spatula to press the purée through a mesh strainer to remove the seeds and extract as much liquid as possible; you should end up with about 1½ cups of seedless purée. Whisk in the soymilk and vinegar, and set aside.

Soften the margarine by beating it in your stand mixer, and then cream it together with the sugar. In a separate bowl, sift the flour and stir in the baking powder, soda, and salt. Add this dry mixture into the stand mixer in about three additions, adding in the raspberry mixture after each addition. Incorporate the vanilla last and mix until just combined, ignoring any small lumps or graininess that may remain. Divide the batter evenly between the two pans; tap them each gently on the counter to remove air bubbles. Bake for 24–30 minutes, until lightly browned all over and a toothpick inserted into the center comes out clean. Although they may just look brown now, don't worry—the cakes will look much redder when sliced. Let cool completely before turning out and frosting.

This frosting is made over the stove, so get out a medium saucepan and whisk together the cornstarch and soymilk, being sure to get out any lumps. Set it over a medium flame and bring it to a boil, whisking occasionally, until it feels significantly thickened. Turn off the heat, place a piece of plastic wrap directly on the surface, and thoroughly chill before proceeding.

Once the puddinglike base is cool, cream together the margarine and sugar in your stand mixer until homogeneous. Add in the base and vanilla and whip on high speed for 2–3 minutes, scraping down the sides of the bowl as needed, until light and fluffy. Frost cake as desired and decorate with fresh blueberries to complete the color scheme.

ROASTED APRICOT ICE CREAM WITH ALMOND PRALINE RIPPLE

Makes About 1 pint

Roasting fruits and toasting nuts intensifies their flavor, allowing their unique characteristics to shine through, even when mixed into a chilly application that can otherwise dull flavors. If you're in a hurry or can't wait to tame your ice cream appetite, you could leave the apricots as they are and substitute 1 cup of almond butter for the praline ripple, but in my opinion the incredible caramel essence you'll get with this recipe as written is more than worth the extra effort.

Almond Praline Ripple:
½ Cup Whole Almonds
½ Cup Granulated Sugar
¼ Cup Water
1 Teaspoon Light Corn Syrup
½ Teaspoon Salt

1 Tablespoon Olive Oil

Roasted Apricot Ice Cream
1 Pound Fresh Apricots
1 Tablespoon Olive Oil
¾ Cup Coconut Milk

½ Cup Dark Brown Sugar, Firmly Packed
1 Teaspoon Vanilla Extract
1 Tablespoon Amaretto

First, you'll want to make the almond praline ripple. Start by combining the sugar, water, and salt into a small saucepan and placing it on the stove over medium heat. Cook the mixture for about 10–12 minutes, until it caramelizes and turns a deep amber color. Quickly stir in the almonds to coat and pour everything out onto a Silpat. Let it cool completely before breaking it into pieces and processing into a smooth paste. Drizzle in the oil, and it should become the consistency of somewhat runny peanut butter. Cover and let rest in the fridge while you make the ice cream.

Preheat your oven to 400°F and lightly grease a sheet pan.

Wash and thoroughly dry your apricots before slicing them in half and removing the pits. Place the halves with the cut sides up on your prepared pan, and drizzle them all with the oil. Roast them for about 20 minutes, until they are so tender that they can scarcely hold themselves together anymore.

Let the apricots cool a bit before scooping them all into your food processor and puréeing them. Once smooth, add in the coconut milk, sugar, vanilla, and amaretto, processing to combine. Chill the mixture thoroughly in your fridge before freezing it in your ice cream maker per the manufacturer's directions.

After freezing in the machine, pour the ice cream out into a plastic tub and drizzle the almond praline paste on top. Use a spatula to marble it in, cover, and quickly move it into your freezer so that it can solidify.

S'MORES PIE

Makes 10–12 servings

S'mores . . . just the word gets me excited! Gooey, toasted marshmallows on top of melted chocolate, all smashed together between two crunchy graham crackers—what's not to love?

Graham Cracker Crust:
1½ Cups Graham Cracker Crumbs
3 Tablespoons Margarine or Coconut
  Oil, Melted
2 Tablespoons Brown Rice Syrup

Chocolate Ganache Filling:
8 Ounces Semisweet Chocolate,
  chopped
1 Cup Coconut Milk

Marshmallow Topping:
¼ Cup Ener-G Egg Replacer
½ Cup Water
1 Teaspoon Vanilla Extract
Pinch Salt
½ Cup Granulated Sugar

Preheat your oven to 350°F and lightly grease a 9-inch round pie pan.

Place the graham cracker crumbs in a medium bowl and pour over the melted margarine or coconut oil and brown rice syrup. Stir thoroughly to moisten all of the crumbs, and then move the mixture into your pie pan. Use lightly moistened hands to press it down into an even layer covering the bottom on sides. Bake for 10–15 minutes, until barely browned around the edges.

While the crust bakes, pour the coconut milk into a microwave-safe bowl and let it heat just to the point of boiling. Dump the chocolate into the coconut milk, and let sit for two minutes so that it can melt. Stir thoroughly until the mixture is completely smooth, mixing until all the lumps are gone. Pour the ganache into your baked crust and carefully move the pie into your refrigerator. Chill thoroughly for at least 1 hour, until the filling is firmly set.

In the bowl of your stand mixer, combine the Ener-G, water, and vanilla, and start mixing on low speed. Scrape down the sides to make sure you aren't missing any of the powder, and increase the speed so that you start to get a nice froth going. Slowly sprinkle in the salt and sugar while the motor is running, and then turn it up all the way to the highest setting. Whip continuously for about 15 minutes, until substantially increased in volume, light, and fluffy. Pour over the layer of ganache, and for best results when cutting, toss the whole pie into the freezer for at least 2 hours before serving.

Once frozen, run it under the broiler for just 5 minutes or so, until the marshmallow topping is golden brown. You could also use a kitchen torch for this step if you'd prefer.

Note: Happily, there are a number of gelatin-free marshmallows on the market these days, so feel free to pick up an 8- or 10-ounce package, or use commercial Ricemellow Creme, instead of making the topping from scracth. If using marshmallows, cut them into smaller pieces if necessary, and evenly distribute them over the top of the pie. Run the whole thing under the broiler as instructed above, and enjoy the toasted, gooey topping while still hot!

SUNNY-SIDE-UP APRICOT DANISHES

*Makes 6
Danishes*

The ultimate breakfast indulgence is definitely the buttery pastries known as Danishes. Not nearly as flaky as puff pastry but not as fussy to make either, the dough does take a serious investment of time, though not much labor. Should you prefer not to go through the hassle of making the pastry from scratch, you can also seek out vegan puff pastry at your local grocery store. The end results won't be nearly as good as with the homemade dough, but you will still get perfectly delicious pastries, and in half of the time. The choice is up to you, and you really can't lose either way.

Danish Dough:

3 Tablespoons Flaxseeds
2 Cups All-Purpose Flour
1 Package Active Dry Yeast
1 Tablespoon Granulated Sugar

1 Tablespoon Lemon Zest
½ Teaspoon Salt
1 Cup Plain Non-Dairy Milk
½ Cup Non-Dairy Margarine
½ Cup Vegetable Shortening

Crème Topping:

4 Ounces "Cream Cheese"
1 Tablespoon Maple Syrup
½ Teaspoon Vanilla Extract
Pinch Salt
3 Fresh Apricots

Begin by grinding your flaxseeds down to a fine powder, and place the resulting meal into a large bowl along with the flour, yeast, sugar, zest, and salt. Pour in the soymilk and mix well to form a homogeneous cohesive dough. Turn it out onto a well-floured surface and knead by hand for about 10 minutes, until smooth. Use a rolling pin to roll it out into a square, about ¼ inch in thickness. Cream the margarine and vegetable shortening together until smooth and spread over the surface of the entire square. Fold the dough into thirds like you would a letter and turn it 90°F. Roll it into a square again and fold it into thirds once more. You have just completed two turns—now the dough needs to rest in the fridge for 2 more hours for the gluten to relax and layer of fat to solidify. After that time has elapsed, give the dough another turn, roll it into a square, and fold it in thirds. Set it back in the fridge and repeat the process once more. Chill the dough before using; you can let it sit in the fridge for a day or two in advance.

When you're ready to bake your Danishes, preheat your oven to 350°F and line a baking sheet with parchment paper or a Silpat.

Prepare the topping by simply mixing together all of the ingredients until smooth. Set aside.

Pull the dough out of the fridge and roll out into a 14- to 16-inch rectangle. Cut it into 6 equal squares and spoon a dollop of the crème in the center of each. Slice the apricots in half, remove the pits, and place them with the cut sides down on top of the crème.

Move the Danishes onto your prepared sheet and let come to room temperature before baking (about 30 minutes). Bake for 25–30 minutes, until the pastry is golden brown. Let cool on a wire rack for at least 15 minutes before serving.

TOASTED COCONUT KEY LIME ICE CREAM

Makes approximately 1 Pint

Believe it or not, this recipe was actually the result of a happy accident. Originally intended to become a pie filling, I hadn't actually taken into account how much the piecrust would hold and was upset at first to discover that it wouldn't all fit. Not one to toss perfectly good food, I decided to make a few more small tweaks to the remainder and then churn it into ice cream. Unsurprisingly, I ended up loving the ice cream even more than the pie, so if you're in the mood for either coconut or key lime pie, don't even bother with the graham crackers or pie dough—make this frozen treat instead!

1 Cup Unsweetened Coconut Flakes
1 13.5-Ounce Can Coconut Milk
1 Cup Granulated Sugar
¼ Cup Cornstarch

Zest and Juice of 4 Key Limes (about 2–3 Tablespoons Zest and ⅓ Cup Juice)
½ Cup Non-Dairy Milk

First, you'll want to toast the coconut in a dry pan to bring out as much nutty flavor as possible. Place a medium skillet over moderate heat and add in all of the coconut flakes. Once they begin to brown, the process will go very fast, so don't step away from the stove. Continue stirring until all of the flakes are more or less evenly browned, and highly aromatic. Immediately move the coconut into a separate bowl to cool so that it doesn't just sit around in the hot pan and burn.

Moving on to the liquid part of the ice cream base, combine the coconut milk, sugar, and cornstarch in a medium saucepan, and whisk vigorously to combine, making sure to beat out any lumps of starch. Once smooth, add in the lime zest and juice, nondairy milk, and your toasted coconut. Mix well and move the pan onto the stove.

Cook it over medium heat for about 10–15 minutes, stirring occasionally, until it just comes to a boil and feels significantly thickened. Set aside and let cool to room temperature before moving it into the fridge. Allow it to chill for at least 30 minutes, but the colder the better.

Freeze using your ice cream maker according to the manufacturer's directions.

TRUE BLUE BUNDT CAKE

Makes 16–18 servings

Feeling blue? Another helping of blue could actually help cheer you up, at least if it's this deep blue cake! Blueberries are puréed and added into the batter to give this bundt all-over color, and then chewy dried blueberries are tossed in to add bursts of sweet berry flavor. Fresh blueberries could also take the place of dried, if unavailable, but be sure to coat them in flour and fold them in gently so that they don't sink straight to the bottom.

1 Cup Non-Dairy Margarine	1 Tablespoon Lemon Juice	⅛–¼ Teaspoon Cinnamon
1½ Cups Granulated Sugar	1½ Cups All-Purpose Flour	½ Teaspoon Salt
¼ Cup Dark Brown Sugar	1 Cup Whole Wheat Pastry Flour	¾ Cup Dried Blueberries
¾ Cup Non-Dairy Milk	2 Teaspoons Baking Powder	2 Cups Fresh or Frozen Blueberries

Preheat your oven to 325°F and lightly grease and flour a bundt pan.

Begin by creaming together the margarine and both sugars in a stand mixer. It can sometimes take a while depending on how soft your margarine is, but don't be tempted to rush this process, as it's critical to the texture of your finished cake. Meanwhile, combine the soymilk and lemon juice and set aside.

In a separate bowl, sift together both flours, baking powder, cinnamon, and salt. Toss in the dried blueberries and make sure they're nicely coated so that they don't sink to the bottom of your cake.

Using a blender or food processor, thoroughly purée your fresh or frozen blueberries. The finer the better; you can even choose to strain out the resulting pulp if you'd like, but I think it adds more flavor. Pour in the soymilk and lemon mixture and pulse briefly to combine.

Slowly add in part of the dry mix into your stand mixer, let it begin to incorporate, and follow it with a portion of the liquid. Alternate between the two until both are completely used up, allowing the mixer to catch up with your demands before proceeding. Pour the batter into your prepared bundt pan, tap it a few times on the counter to bring any air bubbles up to the surface, and smooth out the top. Bake for 60–70 minutes, until browned around the edges and a toothpick inserted into the center of the ring comes out clean. Let cool in the pan for at least 20 minutes before unmolding.

WATERMELON BOMBE

Serves 8–10

For many years, special summer occasions called for one cake and one cake only: the watermelon roll. Composed not of cake but of ice cream, it was something that came from one well-known restaurant, and was impossible to replicate at home . . . or so I thought. Many years later, I was determined to revive this childhood favorite, and in doing so, discovered that it was far superior to that chemical- and artificial color-laden original. It's still only for special occasions, since it takes quite a bit of work to put all of the layers together, but I've never enjoyed any ice cream cake more.

Mint Ice Cream:
1½ Cups Plain Non-Dairy Milk
⅓ Cup Fresh Mint Leaves, Lightly
    Packed
½ Cup Granulated Sugar
2 Teaspoons Cornstarch
Pinch Salt
½ Teaspoon Vanilla Extract

1 Ripe Avocado
1 Teaspoon Lemon Juice

Vanilla Ice Cream:
1 Cup Plain Soy or Coconut Creamer
2 Teaspoons Cornstarch
¼ Cup Granulated Sugar
1 Teaspoon Vanilla Extract

Watermelon Sorbet:
2½ Cups (20 Ounces) Watermelon
    Purée
2 Tablespoon Lemon Juice
1 Cup Granulated Sugar
¼ Cup Miniature Semisweet
    Chocolate Chips, or Finely
    Chopped Semisweet Chocolate

Line a 1½-quart bowl with plastic wrap and try to keep it as flat against the sides as possible, leaving a good bit of overhang. Set aside.

The first layer you need to make is the mint, which will create the green rind. Combine the soymilk and mint leaves in a medium saucepan over medium heat, and bring the liquid just to the brink of boiling. Turn off the heat and cover the pot; let steep for at least 20 minutes, or up to 45 for a more intense flavor. Strain out the spent mint leaves and return the soymilk to the stove. Stir the cornstarch into the sugar before adding both into the pot, and turn the heat back on to medium. Stir occasionally until the sugar has dissolved and the liquid comes back to a boil. Remove from the stove, stir in the salt and vanilla. Place a piece of plastic wrap directly on the surface of the mixture and thoroughly chill in the fridge. Once the base is cooled and ready to go, purée your avocado along with the lemon juice until completely smooth, and mix it into your cooked soymilk. Freeze in your ice cream maker according to the manufacturer's instructions, and then smooth it along the sides of your plastic-lined bowl. Use a smaller bowl to even out the insides, and immediately move it into the freezer to harden.

Next up is the white membrane, which is easy to make. Place the soy creamer in a small saucepan, combine the cornstarch with the sugar, and then add both as well. Whisk every now and then until it comes up to a full boil, and then take it off the heat. Place plastic wrap on the surface of the cooked custard and chill thoroughly. It's critical that this mixture is cooled all the way through, since it won't go through the ice cream machine. Take the bowl lined with the mint ice cream out of the freezer and pour the vanilla custard in. Tilt the bowl around in circles to coat the insides evenly, and then pour out any excess that refuses to stick. Put the bowl back in the freezer as soon as you're done.

Finally, it's time to make the "flesh."

Mix together the watermelon purée, lemon juice, and sugar in a medium saucepan, and place over medium heat. Cook just until the sugar has dissolved. Thoroughly chill before processing in your ice cream maker per the manufacturer's directions, and toss in the mini chips or chopped chocolate in the last 5 minutes of churning. Smooth the sorbet into the center of your frozen shell, and return it to the freezer again for at least 4 hours, or until ready to serve.

Pull the "melon" out by grabbing hold of the overhang and using it as leverage. Place it with the open side down on a serving plate, and peel the plastic off of the sides. Slice and serve. Just remember to keep the extra in the freezer so that it doesn't melt in the summer heat!

Note: Like this idea but don't have the time to make each individual ice cream? No sweat! Just soften 1 pint of any green vegan ice cream that you enjoy (lime, avocado, mint, pistachio, matcha, etc.), ½ pint of vanilla, and 1½ pints of red sorbet (raspberry, strawberry, red currant, etc.) and assemble as directed. You could also make a yellow or orange-fleshed watermelon instead (lemon, mango, orange, etc.).

TOMATO CAKES WITH BALSAMIC FROSTING

Makes 15–16
Cupcakes

Tomato soup cakes have been around since the turn of the century as a thrifty way of making something sweet in the times of rationing. Originally dubbed "mystery cake" as a way of concealing the secret ingredient, perhaps acknowledging that unwitting diners might be scared off by the novel concept, the processed tomato product was merely an extender, filling in the bulk of the cake without using eggs, only to be covered up in heavy gingerbread-like spices. You'd never know there was ever a tomato present in the tender crumb, which is both the beauty and tragedy of this classic recipe.

Taking inspiration from these humble origins but with the desire to celebrate the bold, beautiful tomatoes now in season rather than bury them in an avalanche of sugar, it seemed high time to revisit the idea of a tomato cake. At last, you can truly taste the tomato in these fiery red cupcakes. Not only that, but the unassuming beige frosting holds yet another surprise taste sensation: A tangy punch of balsamic vinegar, tempered by the sweetness of the rich and fluffy matrix that contains it. Trust me, it's one of those crazy things that you've just got to taste to believe. Although it may sound like an edible acid burn, that small splash is just enough to brighten up the whole dessert.

Tomato Cupcakes:
2 Cups Diced Fresh Tomatoes,
    Roughly Blended, or 1 14-Ounce
    Can Crushed Tomatoes
⅓ Cup Olive Oil
⅓ Cup Dark Brown Sugar, Firmly
    Packed
1 ½ Cups All Purpose Flour
½ Cup Granulated Sugar
1 Teaspoon Baking Powder

½ Teaspoon Baking Soda
½ Teaspoon Salt
½ Teaspoon Ground Ginger
¼ Teaspoon Ground Nutmeg
⅛ Teaspoon Ground Black Pepper

Balsamic Frosting:
½ Cup Margarine
2 Cups Confectioner's Sugar
1 Tablespoon Balsamic Reduction or
    Balsamic Glaze
1 Teaspoon Vanilla Extract
Up to 1 Tablespoon Plain Non-Dairy
    Milk

Preheat your oven to 350 degrees and line 15 – 16 cupcake tins with papers.

Combine the blended (but not completely pureed) tomatoes, olive oil, and brown sugar in a medium bowl. Stir until the sugar has dissolved and set aside.

In a separate large bowl, whisk together the flour, granulated sugar, baking powder and soda, salt, and spices. Make sure that all the dry goods are thoroughly distributed before adding in the wet ingredients. Mix everything together with a wide spatula, stirring just enough to bring the batter together and beat out any pockets of unincorporated dry ingredients. A few remaining lumps are just fine.

Distribute the batter between your prepared cupcake pans, filling them about three-fourths of the way to the top. Bake for 17 – 20 minutes, or until a toothpick inserted into the centers pulls out cleanly, with perhaps just a few moist crumbs clinging to it. Do not wait for the tops to brown because the centers will be thoroughly overcooked by then. Let cool completely before frosting.

To make the frosting, place the margarine in the bowl of your stand mixer fitted with the whisk attachment. Beat briefly to soften before adding in the confectioner's sugar, balsamic glaze, and vanilla. Begin mixing on low speed until the sugar is mostly incorporated, pausing to scrape down the sides of the bowl as needed. Turn the mixer up to high and slowly drizzle in non-dairy milk as needed to bring the whole mixture together. Continue whipping for about 5 minutes, until light and fluffy. Apply to cupcakes as desired.

AUTUMN

APPLE SPICE SCROLLS

Makes 12–14 scrolls

Across between a cookie and a pastry, these are both soft, crisp, and just a touch gooey all at the same time. Sturdy yet tender dough holds in soft, supple apple spread, infused with cider, spices, and toothsome chunks of whole apple. Only modestly sweetened, they make for an excellent breakfast option on cozy autumnal mornings. Just pop one or two in the toaster oven until warm and lightly crisped and you'll have the typical toaster pastry beat by a mile. If your sweet tooth prefers things with a bit more sugar, feel free to throw a quick glaze on top, but I don't think they need anything more.

Spiced Apple Filling:
2 Cups Dried Apple Rings, Chopped
1½ Cups Apple Cider or
　　Unsweetened Apple Juice
1 Cup Unsweetened Apple Sauce
1 Teaspoon Ground Cinnamon
½ Teaspoon Ground Ginger

¼ Teaspoon Ground Allspice
¼ Teaspoon Ground Nutmeg
Yeasted Pastry Dough:
2½ Cups All-Purpose Flour
1 Teaspoon Active Dry Yeast
½ Teaspoon Lemon Zest
¼ Teaspoon Salt

¼ Cup Non-Dairy Milk, at Room
　　Temperature
¼ Cup Dark Brown Sugar, Firmly
　　Packed
¼ Cup Olive Oil
¼ Cup Apple Butter
2–3 Tablespoons Water

The filling should be at room temperature or cooler before the scrolls are baked, so it's best to prepare it first. To do so, place your chopped dried apple pieces, cider, applesauce, and spices in a medium saucepan, and bring to a boil over medium heat. Reduce the heat to medium low and simmer the mixture for about 20 minutes, stirring every now and then, until almost all of the liquid has been absorbed. Use an immersion blender to pulverize it right in the pot, or transfer the apple filling into your food processor or blender. Pulse or blend just until you get a thick, chunky paste, somewhat like a rough apple butter. Let cool—set the mixture in the fridge if you want to speed up the cooling process.

For the pastry dough, preheat your oven to 350ºF and line a baking sheet with a Silpat or piece of parchment paper.

Place the flour, yeast, zest, and salt in the bowl of your stand mixer. These pastries aren't really leavened, but include yeast for flavor, so it doesn't need to be proofed beforehand. Mix everything together until well combined and set aside.

In a separate bowl, whisk together the nondairy milk, sugar, oil, apple butter, and 2 tablespoons of water. Pour this liquid mixture into your bowl of dry ingredients and mix with the paddle attachment until just combined. You should end up with a thick, stiff, but soft dough. If it doesn't quite come together, add in 1 additional tablespoon of water and mix again. Allow the dough to rest for 15 minutes for the gluten to relax, but not long enough for it to begin to rise.

On a lightly floured surface, turn out the dough from the bowl and use your hands to pat it out into a rough rectangle shape. Lightly flour the top to make sure it doesn't stick to the rolling pin, and roll it out to approximately 12 × 14 inches in dimension. Spread your cooled filling out all over the rectangle, but go lighter on the long ends to make sure it doesn't all end up in the center once rolled.

Gently roll up each of the long sides so that they meet in the center, forming what looks like a very long scroll. Cut 1-inch-wide slices with a very sharp knife, using a sawing motion but not pressing down too hard, so as not to squish the filling out of the dough. Transfer the scrolls to your prepared baking sheet with one of the cut sides down, and bake for 25–30 minutes, until lightly browned around the edges. Let cool before serving.

BLACK CAT COOKIES

Yield = variable, depending on size of cookie cutter

On All Hallows' Eve, the last thing you would want is for a jet-black cat to cross your path, cursing you with bad luck. These black cat cookies, on the other hand, would be a welcome surprise! The dark intensely chocolate batter is no average sugar cookie dough either and is sure to satisfy the most die-hard chocoholics. Sure, you can make them in any shape at any time of the year, but they always make a big impression when served on Halloween.

1 Cup Non-Dairy Margarine
1¼ Cups Granulated Sugar
2¾ Cups All-Purpose Flour

¾ Cup Dutch-Processed Cocoa Powder
3 Tablespoons Black Cocoa Powder
½ Teaspoon Salt

½ Teaspoon Baking Powder
⅓ Cup Cold Coffee
1 Teaspoon Vanilla Extract

Use your stand mixer to thoroughly cream the margarine and sugar together. In a separate bowl, sift the flour, both cocoa powders, salt, and baking powder, stirring well to combine. Add about half of these dry ingredients into the mixing bowl, processing it until fully incorporated. Pour in the cold coffee and vanilla, along with the remaining flour mixture. Continue to mix until it forms into a smooth homogeneous dough. Form the dough into a ball, flatten it out a bit, wrap in plastic, and chill for at least 1 hour before proceeding.

After the dough has had time to rest in the refrigerator, start heating your oven to 350°F.

On a lightly floured surface, roll out the dough to about ¼–⅛ of an inch in thickness. Use cat-shaped cookie cutters to shape the cookies and place them on baking sheets lined with Silpats or parchment paper. Use a toothpick to poke in eyes and whiskers, if desired. Brush the excess flour off the cookies, but don't go crazy if it still has a light coating—most of it will bake off.

Bake for about 8–14 minutes, depending on the size. It's tough to judge when these cookies are done because they're so dark to begin with, but the edges should be firm and the centers soft and slightly puffed up.

Cool completely on a wire rack before storing in an airtight container at room temperature.

BLUSHING APPLE SORBET OR GRANITA

Makes approximately 1 Pint

When it comes to apples, it seems as though everything possible has already been done with them. From apple cakes to apple pies, apple chips to apple dumplings, this ubiquitous fruit has the peculiar disadvantage of being overloved, and overused. Determined to find a new life for such a common fruit, I created this chilly sorbet. Shower apples with a healthy dose of wine and the color returns to their cheeks, renewing their spirit and essence. At a time when there's much to celebrate, this sorbet is definitely something invigorating to toast with—and to!

2 Cups Red Wine
½ Cup Apple Juice Concentrate

¼ Cup Maple Syrup

2 Tart Green Apples, Peeled, Cored, and Sliced

In medium sauce pan, simply combine the wine, apple juice concentrate, and water. Set it over a medium flame and bring it to a boil. Reduce the heat and simmer for about 10 minutes before adding in the apples. Cook for an additional 15 minutes or so, until the apples become tender and are practically falling apart. Turn off the heat, let the contents of the pot cool down a bit, and purée the apples using either a submersion blender or by transferring it to a traditional blender. Strain the resulting liquid to remove any fibrous bits and chill the resulting mix thoroughly in the refrigerator before freezing as instructed by your ice cream manufacturer's directions.

If you would prefer to make a granita, instead of using an ice cream maker, pour the sorbet base into a large baking dish and place on a flat surface in your freezer. Wait for about 1 hour for ice crystals to begin forming, and scrape the surface with a fork to break them up. Return the pan to the freezer, and repeatedly scrape up the newly formed ice crystals at intervals of about 30 minutes. Once there is no more liquid and you have a fairly fine snowy mixture (approximately 2–3 hours), serve immediately.

BUTTERNUT VANILLA BEAN PANCAKES

Serves 4–6

Easily my favorite weekend breakfast, there's nothing quite like waking up to the luscious aroma of coffee and sweetness wafting from the kitchen. Piling up a big stack of soft, fluffy pancakes and drenching them in about a gallon of maple syrup as a kid, it was breakfasts like these that made waking up before noon worthwhile. Though they were reserved only for the most special ocassions, and usually when we had company, I relished every bite when they graced the breakfast table. Though I'm happy enough to take them any which way—with chocolate chips, blueberries, plain—I've recently fallen in love with a more autumnal version, infused with the delicate sweetness of butternut squash and vanilla bean. Though it's hard to turn down the maple syrup, which still makes a fine match with these little griddle cakes, I've found that an even more unique treat comes from reduced and spiced apple cider, bringing with it a slightly tart punch in addition to a syrupy sweetness. Since it takes a bit longer to prepare, I'd advise making it the night before, because no one will want to wait that long before devouring these pancakes!

Chai-Spiced Cider Syrup:
4 Cups Apple Cider
1 Teaspoon Chai Spice**
2 Teaspoons Cornstarch
1 Tablespoon Maple Syrup

Butternut Pancakes:
2 Cups White Whole Wheat Flour
1 Tablespoon Flaxseeds, Ground
½ Teaspoon Salt
2 Teaspoons Baking Powder
1 Teaspoon Baking Soda
1 Cup Lightly Mashed, Roasted
   Butternut Squash*

2 Tablespoons Dark Brown Sugar,
   Firmly Packed
1 Tablespoon Tahini
1⅔ Cups Plain Non-Dairy Milk
2 Teaspoons Apple Cider Vinegar
3 Tablespoons Olive Oil
1 Vanilla Bean
Pinch Ground Nutmeg

To make the cider syrup, place the apple cider and chai spice in a medium sauce pan over medium-low heat, whisk well, and simmer until reduced to 1 cup, approximately 60 minutes. Stir the cornstarch and maple syrup together to create a thick paste, and mix that into the syrup. Whisk thoroughly to incorporate, and continue to cook for another 5 minutes or so until the mixture has thickened. Let cool completely and store in the fridge in an air-tight glass jar or bottle.

For the pancakes, begin by mixing the flour, ground flaxseeds, salt, baking powder and soda together in a large bowl.

In a separate bowl, whisk together the mashed butternut squash, sugar, tahini, non-dairy milk, vinegar, and olive oil until smooth. Slice the vanilla bean in half lengthwise, and use the edge of the knife blade to scrape out the seeds inside. Add them to the wet mixture, along with the nutmeg.

At this point, you can start preheating a medium non-stick skillet over moderate heat. You'll know it's ready when you can splash a small drop of water on it, and the droplet will sort of skitter around on top. If it just sits there, the pan is too cold, but if it immediately sizzles off, the pan is too hot.

Once the skillet it hot and ready, pour the wet ingredients into the bowl of dry, and combine the two by mixing with a wide spatula, stirring as little as possible to bring together a loose batter. Spoon ladlefuls of about ¼ cup per pancake into the skillet, and cook no more than 3–4 at a time, depending on how large your pan is. Allow the pancakes to cook, undisturbed, for about 3–4 minutes before gently lifting up one edge to check if the bottom is appropriately browned. There should be bubbles bursting on top, and the edges should be mostly firm. If they seem cooked on the bottom, flip them over, and cook for another 3–4 minutes until similarly browned on the other side.

Slide the pancakes out onto a waiting plate, and repeat with the remaining batter. If you want to keep them hot and serve them all at once, stash them in your oven set to the "warm" function, or preheated to about 200°F. Just be mindful of your time and keep them in there for no more than 30 minutes, or the pancakes will dry out.

*To roast your butternut, preheat the oven to 400°F, and peel, gut, and cube your squash. Lightly coat with oil and spread onto a baking sheet. Bake for about 30–45 minutes, until the edges are golden brown and all of the pieces are fork-tender. Let cool completely, and then roughly mash with a potato masher or ricer.

If you're not up for roasting your own butternut, you could also go ahead and make a pumpkin version of these pancakes by substituting an equal amount of canned pumpkin purée.

**Though mixture of spices to create the illustrious combination known as chai vary greatly between cooks, the proportions that I favor are as follows: 2 tablespoon ground ginger, 1½ tablespoons ground cardamom, 1 tablespoon ground cinnamon, 2 teaspoons ground nutmeg, 2 teaspoons allspice, 1½ teaspoons ground cloves, and 1 teaspoon ground white pepper. Mix well, and store in an air-tight bottle in a cool, dry place.

BUTTERY PECAN ICE CREAM

Makes 1 generous pint

Toasted pecans, browned "butter," rich vanilla custard . . . are you drooling yet? Just wait until all of it is mixed together and churned into a frozen delight. It never gets too cold for ice cream, if you ask me, and this flavor is so perfectly suited to the season that you'll have to agree too.

¼ Cup Non-Dairy Margarine
1 Cup Pecans, Roughly Chopped
2 Cups Plain Soy or Coconut
    Creamer

½ Cup Plain Non-Dairy Milk
½ Cup Dark Brown Sugar, Firmly
    Packed
½ Teaspoon Salt

2 Tablespoons Cornstarch
½ Teaspoon Vanilla Extract

In a medium saucepan, melt the margarine over low heat. Add in the pecans and sauté for 3–5 minutes, until they begin to release a nutty aroma and turn a deeper brown color. There will seem to be a lot of margarine, but don't worry, as you're not looking for it to be absorbed or completely used up in this stage. Take out two separate bowls and drain the excess margarine into one, and move the toasted pecans into the other. Draining the nuts thoroughly is critical so that they don't become soggy or greasy later on. Set the nuts aside.

Set a medium pot over the stove on medium heat and combine the leftover margarine, soymilk, soy creamer, sugar, salt, and cornstarch. Stir everything together until dissolved, and let the pot cook for a few minutes until the contents come to a steady boil. If the liquid threatens to bubble over, reduce the heat and whisk vigorously while heating for an additional 1–2 minutes, until the mixture feels slightly thicker. Remove from heat and stir in the vanilla. Let cool to room temperature before covering and moving it into your refrigerator to chill for at least 20 minutes.

Once thoroughly chilled, transfer the ice cream base into your ice cream maker and freeze according to the manufacturer's instructions. During the final 5 minutes of churning, add in the pecans.

CANDIED APPLE COOKIES

Makes approximately 2 dozen cookies, depending on size of cookie cutter

Autumn harvests and fall fairs mean one thing when it comes to sweet treats—candied apples. Brittle caramelized sugar clinging to a fresh, crisp apple, all perched upon a stick . . . it's easy to see why everyone likes them so much, whether young or just young at heart. They aren't exactly the perfect food though, as in my experience, the apples tend to be *too* crisp and tough to sink your teeth into. Try using apple-flavored cookies though, and the texture is better than ever. Make up a big batch of these fun cookies for parties or gatherings, and you won't miss those traditional bulky lollipops one bit!

Apple Cookies:
¾ Cup Margarine
1 Cup Granulated Sugar
¼ Cup Unsweetened Apple Sauce
¼ Cup Apple Juice or Apple Cider

½ Teaspoon Vanilla Extract
3 Cups All-Purpose Flour
1 Teaspoon Baking Powder
½ Teaspoon Salt

Candy Apple Glaze:
1½ Cups Granulated Sugar
¼ Cup Light Corn Syrup
½ Cup Pomegranate Juice
1 Teaspoon Ground Cinnamon

Using your stand mixer, cream together the margarine and sugar. Scrape down the sides of the bowl as needed until smooth. Beat in the apple sauce and follow with the juice and vanilla. Don't worry if the mixture looks somewhat curdled or grainy; just let the mixer do its thing and whisk it for a minute or two. Sift in the flour, baking powder, and salt in three additions, allowing enough time for each new cup of dry ingredients to get at least mostly blended in.

Once the dough is completely smooth, press it together with your hands, cover with plastic wrap, and chill for at least an hour before proceeding.

When you're ready to bake the cookies, preheat your oven to 400°F and line two baking sheets with Silpats or parchment paper.

On a lightly floured surface, roll out the dough to about ¼ inch thick and cut out apple shapes with a cookie cutter. Move the cookies over to your prepared sheets and gently insert a lollipop stick where the stem would be, reshaping the cookies with your fingers if they become distorted in the process. Depending on the size of your cookie cutter, bake the cookies for just 6 to 12 minutes—it's a hot oven, so they will go from perfectly soft and golden to crispy and black very quickly; be sure to keep an eye on them the whole time! Cool the cookies completely before glazing.

To make the glaze, whisk together the sugar, corn syrup, pomegranate juice, and cinnamon in a small saucepan over medium heat. Cook until sugar dissolves, stirring occasionally. Insert your candy thermometer and continue to cook, but without stirring now, until the syrup reaches 290–300 degrees. Turn off the heat and begin dipping the apple cookies in gently so as not to tear them off the sticks. Make sure each one is completely covered, and then hold them above the pan for a few seconds to let the excess glaze drip off. Lay each cookie down on a clean piece of parchment or Silpat, and let cool and harden completely before removing.

These cookies are best if served within a day of being made, because the hard sugar glaze will soften the longer that it sits as it takes on moisture very easily. Do not store them in the fridge as this will only speed up the process.

CRANBERRY CUSTARD PIE

Makes 8–10 servings

This pie is a cross between your standard all-fruit and chiffon pie, making it much lighter than the usual dense often-gooey cranberry pastry filling. A delicate balance of sweet, tart, creamy, and crunchy, it's a fantastic pie to serve for Thanksgiving, or any time you can get your hands on fresh cranberries!

Almond Graham Crust:
1¼ Cups Graham Cracker Crumbs
½ Cup Almond Meal
¼ Cup Margarine or Coconut Oil, Melted
2 Tablespoons Orange Juice

Cranberry Custard Filling:
¾ Cup Dark Brown Sugar, Firmly Packed
½ Cup 100 percent Cranberry Juice
1 12-Ounce Package Extra Firm Silken Tofu
1 Teaspoon Lemon Zest
½ Teaspoon Ground Cinnamon
¼ Teaspoon Salt
½ Teaspoon Baking Powder
2 Cups Whole Unsweetened Cranberries, Fresh or Frozen

Orange Crème Topping:
¼ Cup Cornstarch
1 Cup Orange Juice
1 Cup Vegetable Shortening
1 Cup Granulated Sugar
1 Teaspoon Vanilla Extract

Preheat your oven to 350°F and lightly grease a 9-inch round pie pan.

Stir together the graham cracker crumbs and almond meal and drizzle over the melted margarine or coconut oil and orange juice. Stir thoroughly to moisten all of the crumbs and dump the mixture into your prepared pan. Use your hands to press it into an even layer that covers the bottoms and sides. Bake for 8–10 minutes until lightly browned around the edges, and set aside. Turn down the oven to 325°F.

Pull out your food processor or blender and toss in your block of tofu (after draining away the extra liquid, of course). Thoroughly purée the tofu with the brown sugar and cranberry juice so that it's smooth, pausing to scrape down the sides of the bowl as needed. Add in the zest, cinnamon, salt, and baking powder, and blend once again. Finally, add in the cranberries, and pulse to combine. You want to keep the pieces of cranberries fairly large, so just three or four 1-second pulses should probably do the trick. Pour the cranberry filling into the prebaked crust, smooth out the top, and bake for 55–60 minutes. The edges should be set but the center will still jiggle slightly when tapped, much like cheesecake. Let cool to room temperature and then chill for at least 4 hours before serving.

Since cranberries can be quite tart, the cooked crème provides a subtle hint of sweetness to balance out the dessert. It is prepared by simply whisking together the cornstarch and orange juice in a medium pan so that there are no remaining lumps of starch. Set over medium heat and cook until it comes to a boil, whisking constantly. It should become significantly thickened in just a few minutes. Turn off the heat, place a piece of plastic wrap directly on the surface, and refrigerate until entirely cool and set.

Once chilled, the mixture will be like a solidified pudding. Slide it into the bowl of your stand mixer and mix briefly until smooth. Add in the shortening along with the sugar and vanilla, and whip on high speed for a full 5 minutes, until light and fluffy. Add a dollop to each individual slice, or pipe it decoratively over the whole pie.

CITRUS AND SPICE WAFFLES

Makes 6–12 waffles, depending on your iron

To me, the smell of fall is best presented by the humble pomander. Those simple whole oranges stuck with cloves, looking more like round porcupines than potpourri, have an incredibly woodsy yet fresh scent. Even I will admit, however, that the thought of eating one of them is certainly less than appetizing. But that doesn't mean that those perfectly matched flavors must always be so maligned! Combined in this classic breakfast treat, you could hardly think of any better topping than maple syrup to complete the full fall theme. Trust me, they're much tastier than a pomander could ever dream of being! These sweet treats are just as easily served as a unique dessert as they are for breakfast.

2 Cups White Whole Wheat Flour
¼ Cup Granulated Sugar
2 Teaspoons Baking Powder
½ Teaspoon Baking Soda

½ Teaspoon Salt
1 Teaspoon Ground Cloves
2 Cups Orange Juice

6 Ounces Plain Soy or Coconut
    Yogurt
½ Cup Margarine, Melted

Preheat your waffle iron right away, because the batter will come together quickly.

Sift together the flour, sugar, baking powder and soda, salt, and cloves. Combine the orange juice, soy yogurt, and melted margarine in a separate bowl, and stir thoroughly. Simply pour these wet ingredients into the dry, and use a large spatula to gently fold (not stir) everything together. The technique is much like that for making muffins, but you will end up with a wetter batter. Just be careful not to overdo it; a few lumps or streaks are absolutely fine.

When your waffle iron is hot and ready, add in enough batter to fill the cavity and cook for as long as the manufacturer suggests. All irons differ, but I would suggest checking the waffles no earlier than 5 minutes after first closing the press. If you get too impatient, you'll rip the uncooked waffle apart and will end up with a huge mess on your hands—not exactly a nice thing to wake up to for breakfast!

You can make a batch ahead of time as well. Cook them a little bit less than you normally would, let them fully cool on a wire rack, and wrap them up in a plastic bag before tossing them into the freezer. Reheat them in the toaster oven to get a nice crispy texture and brown exterior.

CRANBERRY STREUSEL BARS

*Yields 16–24
bars*

The moment that fresh cranberries return to store shelves, I snag a couple pounds minimum and toss them into the freezer for safekeeping. These little red gems actually hold up very well when frozen and can keep for at least six months with little damage. Nonetheless, I always keep a couple of bags handy to bake with, since nothing perks up those tart bog berries like a good dose of sugar. These bars would be just as well suited for teatime as holiday gift boxes. Just make sure you stock up on cranberries, because you'll want to make batch after batch of them!

Cranberry Filling:
12 Ounces Fresh or Frozen
    Cranberries (3½ cups)
¾ Cup Maple Syrup
¾ Cup Water
Pinch Salt
½ Teaspoon Cardamom

Crust and Streusel:
1 Cup Dark Brown Sugar
1 Cup Whole Wheat Flour
1 Cup All-Purpose Flour
½ Teaspoon Baking Soda
½ Teaspoon Salt
1 Teaspoon Ground Cinnamon

¼ Cup Plain Non-Diary Milk
½ Cup Canola Oil
1½ Cups Rolled Oats
½ Cup Pecans, Chopped

To make the filling, combine the cranberries, maple syrup, and water in a medium saucepan. Bring to a boil over high heat, then reduce to a simmer. Stirring occasionally, cook for about 10–15 minutes, until the berries burst and the mixture thickens. Remove from heat and stir in the salt and cardamom. Set aside.

Preheat your oven to 375°F and grease a 9 × 13–inch baking dish.

In a large bowl, combine the brown sugar, both flours, baking soda, salt, and cinnamon. Add in the non-dairy milk and oil, stirring to moisten all of the dry ingredients. Finally, add the oats and pecans, mixing so that they're well distributed throughout.

Take half of the mixture and place it in your prepared dish, flattening it out into an even layer. Bake for just 10 minutes to form a firm bottom crust. Spread the cranberry filling over the crust right out of the oven, sprinkle the remaining streusel mixture over the top, and return it to the oven for 24–26 minutes, until lightly browned. Cool completely before cutting into bars.

FIGGY-COFFEE PARFAITS

Serves 6–10

It's easy to take for granted the year-round availability of some ingredients, thanks to our modern megamarts and the phenomenon of "supply and demand." It took me nearly 18 years to realize that nuts didn't actually just appear on shelves, but started out growing on trees just like regular produce, and in fact had harvest seasons as well. Shocked to find a tree producing walnuts close to home one fateful autumn day, I marveled that fewer people celebrated the harvest of these delectable and often pricey morsels. Who wants to eat dusty old walnuts that have been sitting on a store shelf all year? Try to seek out fresh nuts for these parfaits and you're sure to taste a difference.

Though you'll end up with far more sponge candy than you can possibly pile into these parfaits, there's no safe way to make it in any smaller of a batch—doing so would result in a potful of burnt sugar. The good news is that there should be no trouble in finding other uses for it, since this unassuming confection is surprisingly addictive all on its own. Try coating medium-sized pieces in chocolate and see how quickly it disappears!

Salted Sponge Candy Crunch:
⅓ Cup Light Corn Syrup or Agave
    Nectar
1 Cup Granulated Sugar
2 Tablespoons Water
½ Teaspoon Salt
2 Teaspoons Baking Soda
2 Teaspoons Water

Coffee-Walnut Mousse:
1 Cup Non-Dairy Milk
3 Tablespoons Cornstarch
2 Teaspoons Instant Coffee Powder
½ Cup Granulated Sugar
½ Teaspoon Vanilla Extract
1 Cup Chopped Walnuts, Toasted

Baked Figs:
1 Pound Fresh Figs
1–2 Tablespoons Granulated Sugar
1–2 Tablespoons Olive Oil

You'll want to make the sponge candy first since it needs sufficient time to cool and harden before it goes into the parfaits. Begin by laying out a Silpat or piece of parchment paper near the stove. Combine the corn syrup or agave, sugar, 2 tablespoons of water, and salt together in a medium saucepan with high sides, and set over medium heat. Stir just to incorporate all of the ingredients, and then keep that spatula out of the mix until the very end, to prevent unwanted crystals from forming.

Continued on next page.

Cook the sugar syrup, swirling the pan gently every now and then to "stir" the contents, until it reaches 300°F, approximately the hard-crack stage. Remove from the heat, and in a separate dish, mix together the baking soda and remaining water so that there are no lumps of soda remaining. Stir this mixture into the hot sugar and be prepared to work very quickly.

The mixture will bubble furiously, and as soon as the baking soda is completely incorporated, pour the molten candy out and onto your waiting Silpat or parchment. **Do not** press it down or spread it out with your spatula, or else you'll knock the bubbles right out of it. Let cool, undisturbed, until it's at room temperature and can be snapped into pieces. Set aside.

The mousse starts out life in the same way you would prepare a cooked pudding; vigorously whisk together the nondairy milk, cornstarch, coffee powder, and sugar in a medium saucepan until no lumps remain. Turn on the heat to medium and cook, whisking occasionally, until the mixture has thickened significantly, about 5–8 minutes.

Transfer the pudding base, still warm but not screaming hot, into your blender or food processor. Add in the vanilla and toasted walnuts, and thoroughly purée until the mixture is silky smooth. It will take longer for a food processor to do the job, so just be patient, and remember to scrape down the sides of the bowl every now and then to keep everything incorporated. Move the silken mousse into a bowl, place a piece of plastic wrap directly on the surface to prevent a skin from forming, and stash it in the fridge. Chill thoroughly before serving, or at least 3 hours.

Preheat your oven to 350°F, and line a baking sheet with parchment paper, aluminum foil, or a Silpat.

Slice the figs in half and arrange them with the cut sides facing up on your prepared baking sheet. Brush them all over with oil so that they're lightly coated, and sprinkle sugar over the tops. Slide the sheet into the oven and bake for 15–20 minutes, until the figs have softened and the sugar on top is caramelized. Let cool.

Once you have all of the components ready, assembly is very quick and easy. For each glass, layer a few spoonfuls of walnut mousse at the bottom, followed by a handful of chopped walnuts and sponge candy pieces, then another few spoonfuls of mousse, and finally top it off with more walnuts, candy, and the baked figs. Repeat in remaining individual glasses.

GINGERBREAD PUMPKIN SEED BRITTLE

It's just not Halloween without carving jack-o'-lanterns, and the resulting seeds that come out of the process are an added incentive to continue this practice. Roasting them plain with a sprinkle of sea salt is plenty tasty, but to really liven things up a bit, try throwing in a bit of spice and molasses—the transformation is fantastically delicious! This candy is simply too good to even consider handing out to trick-or-treaters.

1 Cup Granulated Sugar
2 Tablespoons Water
1 Tablespoon Molasses

1 Cup In-Shell Pumpkin Seeds
1 Teaspoon Ground Cinnamon
½ Teaspoon Ground Ginger

½ Teaspoon Salt
Pinch Nutmeg
Pinch Black Pepper

Set out two Silpats or pieces of parchment paper nearby the stove so that you're ready when the brittle is done.

Place a medium saucepan over moderate heat and combine the sugar, water, and molasses. Cook until the sugar dissolves, and insert your candy thermometer, swirling the pan if necessary but not stirring. Let it continue to cook until it reaches about 300°F, or the hard-crack stage.

Meanwhile, mix together the pumpkin seeds, spices, and salt in a small bowl. When the sugar has come to the correct temperature, remove the thermometer and quickly stir in the seeds and spices. Working quickly, pour the hot candy out onto the two sheets, dividing it as equally as possible. Press down firmly with a spatula to flatten each out further, if desired, and allow the candy to sit for at least 30 minutes, until completely cooled and set before breaking into pieces. Store in an airtight container at room temperature.

GOLDEN SAFFRON POUND CAKE

Serves 10–12

Believe it or not, there really is a saffron season. Beginning in late September, the crocus stigmas are painstakingly plucked by hand, one by one, and then dried for about seven days before they're ready for culinary use. With all of the effort and time that goes into harvesting these fragile strands, it's easy to see why they come with such a large price tag. When you get the real thing, then they deserve to be the center of attention, and this cake is just the way to give them the spotlight.

¾ Cup Plain Non-Dairy Milk

Big Pinch Saffron Threads (about 0.25 g)

⅓ Cup Canola Oil

⅔ Cup Granulated Sugar

6 Ounces Plain Soy or Coconut Yogurt

¼ Teaspoon Salt

3 Cups All-Purpose Flour

½ Teaspoon Baking Soda

1 Teaspoon Baking Powder

1 Teaspoon Apple Cider Vinegar

½ Teaspoon Vanilla Extract

½ Teaspoon Rose Water

¾ Cup Golden Raisins

The night beforehand, gently warm the soymilk for about a minute in the microwave, and stir in the saffron. Cover and let sit out at room temperature to infuse.

The next morning or afternoon, preheat your oven to 350°F and lightly grease a 9 × 5–inch loaf pan.

Pour the saffron soymilk into a large bowl, straining out the threads if desired. I rarely bother since there are so few, and I don't feel that it changes the cake much either way. Add in the oil, sugar, soy yogurt, and salt, whisking thoroughly to combine. Once homogeneous, sift in the flour, baking powder, and soda, and stir just enough to bring everything together, ignoring any small lumps that may form. Lastly, incorporate the vinegar, vanilla, rose water, and raisins, mixing gently with a few large swipes of the spatula, so that the raisins are evenly distributed throughout the batter.

Pour the batter into your prepared loaf pan and bake 40–50 minutes, until a skewer inserted into the center comes out clean. Let the cake sit at room temperature for 10 minutes before turning out and fully cooling on a wire rack.

LICORICE LOVER'S ALMOND BISCOTTI

Makes 2–3 dozen

Very few people are ambivalent about licorice; you either love it or you hate it. Those who aren't fans might actually be converted after trying this sweet cookie, and licorice lovers are sure to be thrilled that this underutilized flavor final gets the spotlight.

2 Cups All-Purpose Flour
1½ Teaspoons Baking Powder
¾ Cup Granulated Sugar
½ Teaspoon Salt

⅔ Cup Chopped Chewy Black
  Licorice Candy
¼ Cup Slivered Almonds
6 Ounces Plain Soy or Coconut Yogurt
2 Tablespoons Almond Butter

1 Teaspoon Almond Extract
½ Teaspoon Vanilla Extract
¼ Teaspoon Anise Extract
2 Tablespoons Non-Dairy Milk

Preheat your oven to 325°F and line a baking sheet with parchment paper or a Silpat.

In a medium bowl, stir together the flour, sugar, baking powder, and salt just to combine. Add in the licorice pieces and almonds, tossing briefly to distribute, followed by the soy yogurt, almond butter, almond extract, and vanilla. Use a wide spatula to incorporate the wet ingredients thoroughly. The mixture will still be rather dry, but it should start to come together into a cohesive ball of dough. Drizzle in 1 tablespoon of soymilk at a time until the dough is no longer dry but not quite sticky.

Divide the dough in half, and shaping each piece on your prepared baking sheet, form the dough into equally sized logs, 2 inches apart from each other and about 1½ inches wide by 8 or 9 inches long. The exact measurements aren't critical, but make sure that the logs are rather skinny and long, and not mounded up higher than an inch or so. If the dough is very sticky and difficult to work with, lightly moisten your hands with water and very gently tap the dough into the shape you want. Bake for 35–40 minutes, until lightly golden brown on top. Remove the biscotti logs from the oven but leave the heat on. Let the loaves cool for at least 15 minutes.

Using a serrated knife, cut the biscotti into ½- to ¾-inch slices and lay them with the cut side down on a fresh piece of parchment or cleaned Silpat. Return them to the oven and bake for another 10–15 minutes, until lightly browned. Flip the biscotti over onto the other cut side and repeat. Let cool completely before removing them from the baking sheet.

NO-BAKE PUMPKIN CRÈME BRÛLÉE

Serves 4

Imagine a light, luscious pumpkin pie, but without the leaden, heavy pastry crust. Add on a crisp, sugary blanket on top that shatters as you plunge your spoon into the dish, and you'll get this fantastic pumpkin crème brûlée. Unlike a standard crème brûlée, though, you don't even need to turn on your oven! Done in a flash and easily doubled for a crowd, it's a fantastic recipe to have up your sleeve when company is coming. Likewise, it can easily be scaled down for a solo treat or romantic dessert for two.

⅓ Cup Plain Non-Dairy Milk
1 Cup Pumpkin Purée
¼ Cup Granulated Sugar
1 Tablespoon Dark Brown Sugar

1 Tablespoon Non-Dairy Margarine
    or Coconut Oil, Melted
1½ Teaspoons Cornstarch
1 Teaspoon Ground Cinnamon

½ Teaspoon Ground Ginger
Pinch Ground Cloves
4–6 Teaspoons Granulated Sugar

Place the soymilk, pumpkin, both sugars, and margarine or coconut oil in medium saucepan over moderate heat and cook gently until the sugar has dissolved. Whisk in starch thoroughly so that no lumps form, and follow it with all the spices. Stirring continuously, cook for about 5–10 minutes until the mixture has slightly thickened and small bubbles have begun to break on the surface. Equally divide the mixture between four 3-ounce ramekins, and tap them gently on the counter to smooth out the top. Let the custard cool to room temperature before moving the ramekins into your refrigerator to chill for at least 3 hours.

When ready to serve, sprinkle a heaping teaspoon of sugar over the top, and brown them either with a small kitchen torch, or under your oven's broiler for a few minutes, keeping an eye on them the whole time so as not to scorch. Allow the caramelized sugar a minute or two to cool and set before serving.

NOT-A-NEWTON FIG TART

Serves 12–14

As I kid, I absolutely abhorred those cardboardlike fig bars that were supposedly a "healthier" choice when it came time for snack. Try as I might to choke them down, the taste was never worth the effort, and it turns out that the benefits were far and few between as well. It certainly wasn't the figs' fault though, as I learned many years later. Finally free of that preservative-laden pastry, fresh figs are a treasure that one can only enjoy for a few short months. Reinventing the bar was simple enough with flavors so inspiring, and everyone can agree that it's a vast improvement, even for those who might have had no qualms with the original.

Brown Sugar Fig Jam:
1½ Pounds Fresh Figs
1 Cup Dark Brown Sugar, Packed
½ Teaspoon Ground Cinnamon
½ Teaspoon Lemon Zest

Crust:
½ Cup Non-Dairy Margarine
½ Cup Granulated Sugar
1 Tablespoon Ground Flaxseeds
1 Tablespoon Natural Cocoa Powder
1 Cup Almond Meal

1½ Cups All Purpose Flour
¼ Teaspoon Salt
3 Tablespoons Plain Non-Dairy Milk

Toss all of the figs into your food processor or blender and purée them so that you have a mostly smooth mixture. The seeds will still be visible and somewhat lumpy, so there's no need to continue processing it beyond a few minutes.

Move the fig purée into a medium saucepan set over medium heat. Stir in the sugar, cinnamon, and lemon zest, and bring up to a gentle simmer, cooking for about 30 minutes, at which point it should feel somewhat thickened. Set aside and let cool completely.

While the filling cools, preheat your oven to 350°F and lightly grease a 9-inch tart pan with removable bottom.

To make the crust, start by creaming together the margarine and sugar in your stand mixer, adding in the ground flaxseeds and cocoa shortly after. Scrape down the sides of the bowl as necessary so that you have a homogeneous mixture, and add in the almond meal, flour, and salt. Mix for about a minute until mostly combined but still a bit dry, and slowly drizzle in the soymilk. Once you have a smooth dough, gather it into a ball and wrap with plastic. Refrigerate for at least 30 minutes until chilled.

Roll out the chilled crust on a lightly floured surface to about ⅛-inch thickness, and carefully lay it over your prepared pan. The dough is fairly fragile, and more similar to cookie dough than pie dough in texture, so don't panic if it tears while you fit it into the pan. Just use your fingers to press broken pieces back together, and patch any holes with extra scraps of dough. Press it gently into the edges and up the sides, and remove the excess that overhangs the pan. Use a cookie cutter to make shapes out of the scraps to decorate the top of the tart with, if desired.

Once the sides and bottom of the tart pan are evenly covered, pour in the fig mixture and place your decorative pieces of crust over the top in whatever pattern pleases you.

Bake for 30–40 minutes or until the pastry is darkened in color and the filling is softly set. Let the tart cool completely before slicing. Serve with a dollop of whipped cream or a dusting of powdered sugar.

PECAN PRALINE TRIFLE

*Makes 15–20
servings*

Just because a recipe isn't going your way doesn't mean that it can't be saved, and perhaps even elevated beyond your initial idea. Case in point, this trifle: It may have started as a roll cake that cracked beyond repair, but by picking up the pieces and pairing them with a rich, musky pomegranate caramel sauce and fresh red fruits, I could hardly complain about the results. A dollop of ice cream or whipped cream (p 235) lightens up the mixture of flavorful cubes of cake and burnt sugar, but even if eaten completely unadorned, the pecan praline cake is an amazing dessert in itself.

Pecan Praline Cake:
1 Cup Roughly Chopped Pecans
1 Cup Granulated Sugar
¼ Cup Water
1 Teaspoon Light Corn Syrup
¾ Teaspoon Salt
2½ Cups Cake Flour, Divided
¾ Teaspoon Salt

¾ Teaspoon Baking Soda
1 Teaspoon Baking Powder
1 Cup Coconut Milk
¼ Cup Non-Dairy Margarine or
    Coconut Oil, Melted
½ Cup Water
1 Teaspoon Vanilla Extract

Pomegranate Caramel Sauce:
1 Cup Granulated Sugar
Pinch Salt
1 Teaspoon Light Corn Syrup
¾ Cup 100% Pomegranate Juice,
    Divided
2 Tablespoons Non-Dairy Margarine
1 Teaspoon Cornstarch
Fresh Red Currants or Pomegranate
    Arils

The first thing to tackle is the praline. Set out a Silpat or piece of parchment paper near the stove in preparation for the finished product. Place your sugar, water, and corn syrup in a medium saucepan and set over moderate heat. Stir just to moisten all of the sugar, and then keep that spatula far away from that pot! Swirl the pan occasionally to mix, and continue cooking until the sugar has caramelized and turned a deep amber hue—about 10–15 minutes. Pour in the pecans, stir to combine, and cook for just 1 more minute. Turn off the heat and immediately pour the molten sugar and nuts onto your prepared surface. Let sit undisturbed for at least 20 minutes, until cooled and set.

Take this praline and break it up into pieces. Transfer these pieces into your food processor, along with ½ cup of the flour plus the salt, and let it rip. Beware, this is a very noisy process! Keep a close eye on your machine, and stop it once you achieve a fine praline powder. *This can be made a day or two in advance.

Now you're ready to make the cake! Preheat your oven to 375°F and lightly grease and flour a jelly roll pan.

Combine the praline powder and remaining flour in a large bowl, along with the baking powder and soda. In a separate bowl, whisk together the coconut milk, melted margarine, water, and vanilla. Pour the wet ingredients on top of the dry, and use a wide spatula to incorporate the liquids in as few strokes as possible. Pour the resulting batter into your prepared pan and bake for 10–15 minutes. It's a very thin cake and hot oven, so it doesn't take long at all. Just make sure that a toothpick inserted into the center comes out dry. Let the cake cool completely before proceeding to assemble the trifle.

In a small saucepan, combine sugar, salt, corn syrup, and pomegranate juice (reserving 1 tablespoon). Place saucepan over medium heat and cook until sugar dissolves. Once the liquid is no longer grainy, turn the heat to high and bring to a boil. Swirl the pan occasionally, but do not stir. Cook until the mixture reaches 350°F. Then, turn off the heat and stir in the margarine.

In a small bowl, combine reserved pomegranate juice and cornstarch, then add to the pan. Return pan to stove over medium-high heat and bring to a boil, until mixture thickens slightly.

To make the trifle, cut up the cake into small, ½-inch cubes and place half of them on the bottom of a trifle dish or large bowl. Pour a dollop or two of the caramel sauce on top and sprinkle over half of the red currants or pomegranate arils. Add the remaining cake, more caramel, and the last of the pomegranate. Alternatively, you could make individual trifles in small glasses for easy serving. Top with ice cream or whipped cream for a decadent final flourish.

PERSIMMON BLONDIES

Makes 9–12 bars

It wasn't until midway through writing this book that I laid hands on persimmons for the first time in my life. All of the recipes were tested, written, and perfected, but I simply couldn't allow these beautiful fruits to stay out of the picture. Mildly flavored, somewhat like a floral melon and citrus, their unique flavor and orange-reddish color lends incredible depth to the standard chocolate chip blondie.

½ Cup Non-Dairy Margarine
1¼ Cup Dark Brown Sugar, Packed
1 Teaspoon Vanilla Extract
1 Cup Hachiya Persimmon Pulp*

2 Cups All-Purpose Flour
½ Teaspoon Five-Spice Powder
¼ Teaspoon Baking Powder
½ Teaspoon Salt

¾ Cup Semisweet Chocolate Chips, or Dairy-Free White Chocolate Chips
½ Cup Chopped Walnuts (Optional)

Preheat oven to 350°F and lightly grease an 8 × 8–inch square baking pan.

In the bowl of your stand mixer, cream together the margarine and brown sugar thoroughly. Once homogeneous, incorporate the vanilla and persimmon pulp, beating until smooth. Set aside.

In a separate bowl, sift together the flour, five-spice powder, baking powder, and salt, mixing to distribute the dry ingredients evenly. Add in the chocolate chips, tossing to coat, and slowly add this mixture into your stand mixer. Stir just enough to bring the batter together, and then smooth it evenly into your prepared pan. Bake for 30–50 minutes, at least until the edges are lightly browned and the center appears set. That may seem like an awfully wide range, but it depends on whether you prefer an extremely fudgy, almost-underbaked blondie or a firmer, more cakey one.

The blondies may still be slightly gooey in the inside, but they will continue to cook once removed from the oven. Besides, they are "fudgy" bars, so you don't want them to dry out! Wait for the blondies to cool completely before cutting.

*It will take 2 or 3 medium hachiya persimmons to make 1 cup of pulp. They must be completely ripe and squishy before you scrape out the insides, discarding the skin, and purée it in your food processor or blender.

PUMPKIN BUTTER COOKIES

Makes about 32 cookies

Pumpkin cookies sound like a perfect little taste of fall, but everywhere I looked, through books, web pages, and cooking videos, every last recipe produced a fluffy, cakey cookie. While I enjoy a good cakey cookie every now and then, I craved something more crisp, buttery, and shortbreadlike. Requiring less liquid and therefore less pumpkin purée, pumpkin butter is absolutely necessary to provide enough flavor in these miniature squash confections. Delicately flavored, they're a wonderful accompaniment to a hot cup of tea.

½ Cup Pumpkin Butter (page 236)
½ Cup Non-Dairy Margarine
¾ Cup Granulated Sugar

2 ⅔ Cups All-Purpose Flour
4 Teaspoons Cornstarch
1 Teaspoon Ground Cinnamon

¼ Teaspoon Ground Ginger
½ Teaspoon Salt
Pepitas (Hulled Pumpkin Seeds)

First, thoroughly cream together the pumpkin butter and margarine until homogeneous. Beat in the sugar, followed by the flour, cornstarch, cinnamon, and salt. It may seem very dry at first, but resist the temptation to add liquid and continue mixing; it will slowly come together to form a cohesive dough. At that point, press the dough together with your hands to form a smooth ball and wrap it up in plastic. Let it chill in the refrigerator for at least 30 minutes before proceeding.

When the dough is ready to be baked, preheat your oven to 300°F and line two baking sheets with Silpats or parchment paper.

Scoop pieces about the size of walnuts out of the chilled dough, and use the palms of your hands to roll each into a smooth ball, pressing the top down very slightly. To make the lines that mimic those of a real pumpkin's, take a toothpick and press it into the sides at regular intervals. Stick one pepita into the top of each cookie for the "stem" and bake for 13–16 minutes. When the cookies are done, they will be somewhat lightened in color and no longer shiny, but you don't want them to look brown. Let them cool completely on the baking sheets before storing in an airtight container at room temperature.

ROASTED APPLE CHEESECAKE

Makes 12–14 servings

Roasted root vegetables are a favorite of mine in the colder months. The intense, dry heat of the oven brings out all of the sugars and caramelizes them, making for flavorful veggies with a dark, crisp crust on the outside. Applying this same method to fruit is only logical, and is the perfect way to heighten the sweetness of already-delicious produce bound for a dessert. Combining roasted apples with a simple vanilla cheesecake and a spicy gingersnap crust, you end up with a grand finale that's even better than grandma's apple pie. Candied pecans are the "cherry on top" that ties everything together, bringing a satisfying crunch to the whole experience.

Gingersnap Crust:
2 Cups (10 Ounces) Gingersnap Crumbs
¼ Cup Non-Dairy Margarine, Melted

Roasted Apple Filling:
2 Medium Apples
1 Tablespoon Lemon Juice

1 Tablespoon Canola Oil
2 8-Ounce Packages Vegan "Cream Cheese"
½ Cup Granulated Sugar
Pinch Salt
1 Teaspoon Ground Cinnamon
1 Teaspoon Vanilla Extract

Candied Pecans:
1 Tablespoon Non-Dairy Margarine
3 Tablespoons Dark Brown Sugar, Packed
¼ Teaspoon Salt
¼ Teaspoon Ground Cinnamon
¼ Teaspoon Ground Ginger
1 Cup Pecan Halves

Preheat your oven to 400°F and grease a 9-inch springform pan.

To make the crust, simply combine the gingersnap crumbs and melted margarine so that all of the crumbs are moistened, and press it evenly into the bottom of your prepared pan. Set aside.

Peel, core, and slice your apples into wedges about ¼-inch thick. Toss with the lemon juice and oil to prevent them from turning brown or sticking, and spread the pieces out on an ungreased jelly roll pan into an even layer, with none overlapping. Roast for about 10 minutes until fork-tender but not terribly brown. Let cool for a few minutes, and turn down the oven temperature to 375°F. Slide half of the wedges into your food processor, setting the other slices aside. Purée the apple slices and add in the "cream cheese," sugar, salt, cinnamon, and vanilla. Pulse until thoroughly combined and completely smooth, scraping down the sides of the bowl as necessary.

Pour the apple filling over your prepared crust, tapping the pan gently on the counter to remove any air bubbles. Smooth the top down with a spatula and arrange the remaining roasted apple slices around the edges as desired. Bake for

22–26 minutes, until the edges seem set but the center still jiggles a bit when tapped. Let cool to room temperature, and then refrigerate for at least 2 hours before slicing.

For the candied pecans, place a skillet over medium heat and begin by melting the margarine. Once liquefied, add in the brown sugar and cook, stirring occasionally, until dissolved. Add the salt, cinnamon, and ginger; stir to incorporate; and finally mix in the pecans. Stirring constantly, continue to cook the nuts for no longer than 5 minutes, until thoroughly coated with the sugar mixture and smelling nicely toasted. Pour the contents of the skillet out onto a Silpat or piece of aluminum foil and let cool. Pile up the candied pecans in the center of the cheesecake when ready to serve.

ROSH HASHANAH RUGELACH

Makes Approximately 2 dozen cookies

Apples and honey are the traditional treat to celebrate the Rosh Hashanah, in hopes that it will be a sweet New Year. Rolling up a mixture of walnuts, apples, agave, and just a tiny touch of orange blossom water for that floral hint you'd find in honey, the standard buttery rugelach dough becomes a whole lot more special!

Rugelach Dough:
½ Cup Vegan "Cream Cheese"
½ Cup Non-Dairy Margarine
1¼ Cups All Purpose Flour
¼ Teaspoon Baking Powder
Pinch Salt

Apple Filling:
1 Cup Dried Apples, Roughly Chopped
1 Cup Apple Cider
½ Teaspoon Orange Blossom Water
¼ Cup Agave Nectar
¼ Cup Walnuts, Finely Chopped

This dough is very unique, because there's absolutely no sugar in it. This helps to temper the sweetness of the filling, and it also prevents the cookies from browning much. Simply cream the margarine and "cream cheese" together until smooth, and then add in the remaining ingredients. Mix until it comes together in a cohesive dough, being careful not to overdo it; divide it into two pieces and wrap each up in plastic. Let chill for at least 2 hours. Although it may seem like a long time, trust me, you don't want to pull this dough out early. The large proportion of fat to flour makes it extremely finicky when it warms up, so just be patient!

Meanwhile, combine the dried apples, apple cider, and orange blossom water in a medium saucepan. Allow this mixture to simmer for about 10–15 minutes, stirring occasionally, until the liquid has been absorbed. Let cool and transfer it into your food processor or blender, and purée. Add in the agave and pulse to combine. Stir in the nuts by hand so that you don't completely pulverize them in the machine.

When the dough is almost ready to come out of the fridge, preheat your oven to 350°F and line two baking sheets with parchment paper or Silpats.

Take out one portion of the dough and turn it out onto a generously floured surface. Roll it out to about ¼–⅛ of an inch in thickness and try to keep it the shape of a long rectangle. Cut out long triangles, and spread a thin layer of the apple filling on each. Starting with the widest end, roll the triangles up and then pinch them into a slightly rounded crescent shape. Place each finished cookie on your prepared sheet, and repeat with the remaining dough. Bake for 20–30 minutes, until lightly browned.

RUM RAISIN BROWNIES

Makes 9 to 12 brownies

Dark, heavy, robust flavors like rum, dried fruits, and chocolate often remind me of fall and winter, when I crave something more substantial to satisfy my sweet tooth. Adding in some spice certainly helps to sway things in favor of fall, and these brownies just seem to fit the season in my mind. I know that some people may balk at the idea of adding those infernal raisins into something as sacred as a brownie, but trust me on this one—the addition really works here.

¾ Cup Raisins
⅓ + ¼ Cup Rum, Divided
⅔ Cup Canola Oil
2 Tablespoons Molasses
2 Tablespoons Brown Rice Syrup
1½ Cups Granulated Sugar

1 6-Ounce Container Plain Soy or
   Coconut Yogurt
1 Teaspoon Instant Coffee Powder
1 Teaspoon Ground Cinnamon
½ Teaspoon Salt
1 Cup Garbanzo Bean Flour

1 Cup All-Purpose Flour
1¼ Cups Dutch-Processed Cocoa
   Powder
½ Cup Semisweet Chocolate Chips
2 Teaspoons Vanilla Extract

Preheat your oven to 350°F and lightly grease an 8-inch square pan.

In a microwave-safe dish, combine the raisins and ⅓-cup rum and heat on high for 1 minute. Stir to make sure that all of the fruit is moistened, and heat for 1 additional minute. Stir again and cover with plastic to let the fruit rehydrate. Set aside.

Mix together the remaining ¼ cup of rum, oil, molasses, rice syrup, sugar, "yogurt," coffee powder, cinnamon, and salt. Make sure you break up all the lumps of sugar because those can throw off the texture if they go unnoticed.

In a separate bowl, whisk the garbanzo flour, plain flour, and cocoa together. Add the raisins, along with the chocolate chips, into this dry mixture, along with any excess rum, tossing to coat them thoroughly with the flour. This will help prevent them from just sinking to the bottom. Pour the liquid ingredients into the bowl of dry, followed by the vanilla, and stir just enough to completely incorporate everything. Spread your batter into your prepared pan and use a spatula to smooth down the top.

Bake for 30–35 minutes, until the top appears to be mostly set and the insides are still fudgy. Allow the brownies to cool completely before cutting. For best results, freeze the whole pan of brownies to get clean cuts.

Notes: For all you raisin haters, you can swap them out for dried cherries, blueberries, or just more chocolate chips. If using all chocolate, simply use 1 teaspoon of rum extract instead of ⅓ cup of the rum. Since chocolate won't soak up that liquid, leaving the full measure in it would leave you with cakey brownies, rather than fudgy.

STICKY TOFFEE DONUTS

Makes 1–1½ dozen donuts

Take out the napkins and plates—these are seriously decadent donuts that you'll want to eat with a fork. Positively dripping in a sticky sweet glaze, they may be a bit messy, but that's half the fun. When you're in the mood for some sugarcoated comfort, forgoing the fancy or fussy for something a bit homier, these are just the ticket. Similar to the typical sticky toffee pudding, spotted with naturally sweet dates and covered in molasses-like toffee, these are what I crave after a long, cold autumn day.

Sticky Toffee Glaze:
¾ Cup Non-Dairy Margarine
1 Cup Dark Brown Sugar, Firmly
   Packed
½ Cup Granulated Sugar
1 Cup Plain Soy or Coconut Creamer
½ Teaspoon Vanilla Extract
Pinch Salt

Date Donuts:
¾ Cup Plain Non-Dairy Milk
⅓ Cup Dark Brown Sugar, Firmly
   Packed
1¼-Ounce Package Active Dry Yeast
3½–4 Cups All Purpose Flour
1½ Teaspoons Ground Ginger
¾ Teaspoon Salt
1½ Cups Chopped Dates

1 6-Ounce Container Plain Soy or
   Coconut Yogurt
3 Tablespoons Non-Dairy Margarine
   or Coconut Oil, Melted

Approximately 1 Gallon Vegetable Oil
   for Frying

Start out by making the glaze, so it's ready for dipping when the donuts are. In a medium saucepan, begin by melting the margarine over moderate heat, and then add in both sugars and creamer. Bring the mixture to a boil, stirring occasionally, and reduce the heat to low once it reaches a rapid bubble. Let simmer for about 5–10 minutes, until thickened slightly. Stir in the vanilla and salt, and allow the glaze to cool to room temperature.

Moving on to the donuts themselves, warm the non-dairy milk up to about body temperature by microwaving for just about a minute or so. Mix in the sugar, and sprinkle the yeast over the top. Let sit and proof for about 5–10 minutes until bubbly.

In the meantime, assemble your dry ingredients by combining 3½ cups of the flour, the ginger, and salt in the bowl of your stand mixer. Add in the date pieces and toss to coat with the flour and evenly distribute them throughout. Once the yeast has come back to life, pour in the yeast mixture, followed by the yogurt and melted margarine or coconut oil. Employing the hook attachment of the mixer, begin to combine the wet and dry starting on low speed.

Allow the mixer enough time to fully incorporate everything, and if the dough still seems very wet, add in up to an additional ½ cup of flour. Mix for 4–6 more minutes, until the dough is a smooth, slightly sticky ball.

Move the dough ball into a clean, lightly greased bowl, and cover with plastic wrap or a kitchen towel. Let rise in a warm place for about 1 hour, or until it has approximately doubled in size.

Turn out the risen dough onto a well-floured surface, and sprinkle additional flour over the top so that it doesn't stick to the rolling pin. Roll it out to about ¼–½ inch in thickness, and use a 2½-inch round cookie cutter to cut the initial shape. Use a smaller round (about ½–1 inch) shape to cut out the center hole. Use the centers to make donut holes, or add them back into the scraps of dough, re-roll, and cut more large donuts. Let the donuts rest and rise on a lightly oiled piece of parchment paper or a silpat for another 30 minutes.

Prepare to fry by first setting out a wire rack turned upside down on top of paper towels to drain and cool the donuts. On the stove, use a very large, heavy pot with high sides, and make sure that the oil never fills it more than ⅔ of the way to the top, to help prevent splashing and overflow. Always be careful and pay attention to what you're doing when deep-frying, because hot oil burns are no joke. Turn on the heat to medium, and wait for the oil to reach approximately 360–375 ºF. Through the process of cooking, the temperature will vary depending on how many donuts you fry at a time, so be prepared to adjust the flame beneath it as needed.

Once the oil has come up to the proper temperature range, slowly lower in one raw donut at a time using a mesh spider or large slotted spoon. Don't crowd the pot, and only fry 3–4 donuts at a time, at most, so that the oil doesn't suddenly drop in temperature. That would result in a longer cook time and greaser pastries. The donuts will fry very fast; after about 60 seconds, the first side should reach of state of golden brown. Gently flip them over, and then fry the second side for only 30–60 seconds, until similarly browned.

Fish out the finished donuts with the spider or spoon, drain on the overturned rack for at least 5 minutes before handling. Quickly dip each donut in the prepared glaze while still warm, and repeat until all of the donuts are fried and glazed. Serve immediately.

STUFFED CIDER DONUTS

Makes approximately 1½ dozen donuts

Growing up in suburban Connecticut, I've always been lucky enough to have easy access to both the bustling city and quiet farmlands. Though I mostly consider myself a "city girl," come fall, the place to be isn't the noisy and congested metropolis, but the quiet apple orchards with their omnipresent smell of fried cider donuts that wafts through the fields. Delicious in concept but somewhat disappointing in execution, I always craved more apple flavor than those oily rings could ever deliver. Finally, I took to the kitchen and not only infused the dough itself with fresh apple cider, but stuffed each golden brown nugget with a slow-simmered apple filling. Now, that's what fall should taste like!

Cider Donuts:
1½ Cups Apple Cider
¼ Cup Apple Butter
1 Teaspoon Apple Cider Vinegar
¼ Cup Non-Dairy Margarine or Coconut Oil, Melted
3½ Cups All-Purpose Flour
½ Cup Granulated Sugar
2 Tablespoons Flaxseeds, Ground
2 Teaspoons Baking Powder
1 Teaspoon Baking Soda
1 Teaspoon Ground Cinnamon
¼ Teaspoon Ground Nutmeg
½ Teaspoon Salt
⅔ Cup Plain Non-Dairy Milk

Approximately 1 Gallon Vegetable Oil for Frying

Cinnamon-Sugar Coating:
1 Cup Granulated Sugar
1 Tablespoon Ground Cinnamon

Stewed Apple Filling:
3 Cups Finely Diced, Unpeeled Apples (About 2 Medium Fuji)
1 Teaspoon Lemon Juice
⅓ Cup Dark Brown Sugar, Firmly Packed
1½ Tablespoons Cornstarch
½ Teaspoon Ground Cinnamon
¼ Teaspoon Ground Ginger
Pinch Ground Nutmeg
½ Cup Apple Cider

Begin by making the filling so it's cool and ready to go by the time your donuts are done. Combine your diced apple pieces, lemon juice, brown sugar, cornstarch, and spices in a medium saucepan. Toss everything together to coat the apple pieces and evenly distribute the spices and cornstarch. Add the cider and stir well to ensure that there are no lumps of cornstarch remaining. Turn on the heat to low and cook, stirring every few minutes, for 20–30 minutes, until the apple pieces are tender and the liquid has thickened. Remove from the heat and let cool completely before using to stuff your donuts.

Pour the apple cider into a medium saucepan, along with the apple butter and vinegar. Set on the stove over medium-low heat, and gently simmer until the mixture has reduced to a total volume of about ½ cup, about 30 minutes. Turn off the heat and add in the margarine or coconut oil, stirring until it has melted. Set aside and let cool.

Meanwhile, in the bowl of your stand mixer, combine the flour, sugar, ground flaxseeds, baking powder and soda, spices, and salt. Install the paddle attachment for the machine, and once cooled to room temperature, pour in the reduced cider mixture. Mix on low speed, pausing to scrape down the side of the bowl as needed to incorporate the dry goods. Add in the nondairy milk and stir just until combined and you achieve a smooth dough.

Lay out two Silpats or pieces of parchment paper on baking sheets and turn out the dough onto one. Sprinkle the top very lightly with flour and use the palms of your hands to gently flatten it out to about ½ inch in thickness. Move the dough into your freezer and chill for about 30 minutes until very firm. Cut out rounds using a cookie cutter about 2 or 2½ inches in diameter. Transfer the cut donuts onto the second prepared baking sheet and refrigerate for at least 20 minutes before frying. Gather up the dough scraps, press them together, flatten, and cut out more rounds as described above until all the dough is used.

Finally, we're ready to break out the oil! Use a very large heavy pot with high sides, and make sure that the oil never fills it more than ⅔ of the way to the top, to help prevent splashing and overflow. Always be careful and pay attention to what you're doing when deep-frying, because hot oil burns are no joke. Turn on the heat to medium and wait for the oil to reach approximately 360–375 degrees. Through the process of cooking, the temperature will vary depending on how many donuts you fry at a time, so be prepared to adjust the flame beneath it as needed.

While you're waiting for the oil to come up to temperature, mix together the sugar and cinnamon for coating the donuts in a small dish. Set out a wire rack turned upside down on top of paper towels to cool and drain the finished donuts.

To fry your dough rounds, slowly lower in one raw donut at a time using a mesh spider or large slotted spoon. Don't crowd the pot, and only fry 3–4 donuts at a time, at most, so that the oil doesn't suddenly drop in temperature. That would result in a longer cook time and greaser pastries. The donuts will fry very fast; the first side should only take about 60 seconds to reach delicious golden brown color, and then the second a mere 30–60 seconds. Fish out the finished donuts with the spider or spoon, drain on the overturned rack for about 5 minutes, and then toss in the cinnamon sugar while still warm. Repeat with the remaining dough rounds.

Once fried and cooled, the finishing touch is to insert the apple filling. Spoon the cooled filling into a pastry bag fitted with a medium to large round tip—make sure the piping tip you select is big enough to accommodate the apple chunks, but not so large that it will leave a gaping crater in the sides of your donuts. Insert the tip into the side of a donut, and fill just until it seems so full it might burst. Serve as soon as possible, because they're best while still warm.

SWEET POTATO CASSEROLE CUPCAKES

*Makes 12
cupcakes*

While I'm typically against the brown sugar and marshmallow-laden version of sweet potato casseroles, I have to admit that the idea lends itself quite nicely to the dessert course. Vegan marshmallows are still rather hard to come by, but with a generous swirl of maple frosting, you certainly won't miss the extra sugar.

Sweet Potato Cupcakes:
1 Cup Sweet Potato Purée
¼ Cup Plain Non-Dairy Milk
¼ Cup Non-Dairy Margarine, Melted
¼ Cup Granulated Sugar
½ Cup Dark Brown Sugar, Packed
½ Teaspoon Vanilla Extract

1¼ Cups All-Purpose Flour
1 Teaspoon Ground Cinnamon
¼ Teaspoon Ground Ginger
½ Teaspoon Salt
½ Teaspoon Baking Soda
¾ Teaspoon Baking Powder
½ Teaspoon Apple Cider Vinegar

Maple Frosting:
½ Cup Vegetable Shortening
1 Cup Confectioner's Sugar
¼ Cup Maple Syrup
1 Tablespoon Plain Non-Dairy Milk
  (If Needed)

Preheat your oven to 350°F, and line 12 muffin tins with cupcake liners.

Combine the sweet potato, soymilk, margarine, both sugars, and vanilla in a large bowl, stirring until homogeneous. Slowly add in the flour, along with the spices, salt, baking soda, and powder, and mix until just combined, ignoring any small lumps that might remain. Incorporate the vinegar last, and once completely mixed in, divide batter evenly among the cups. Bake for 18–22 minutes, until a toothpick inserted in the center comes out clean. Cool completely on a wire rack before frosting.

To make the frosting, mix together the shortening and sugar in your stand mixer until smooth, and pour in the maple syrup. Whip on high speed for about 5 minutes, adding in the soymilk if it seems too stiff, until the frosting is fluffy but spreadable.

TORTA AL VINO

12–14 servings

Autumn means harvesttime in many parts of the world, and in Italy, champagne grapes are the crowning jewels to a successful growing season. Becoming available as the months begin to grow chilly, they possess an intense sweetness unlike standard grapes. Paired with a fruity red wine to reinforce the flavor, slices of this sophisticated cake could be appropriate for dinner parties, tea breaks, or breakfasts alike. Should these precious fruits of the vine elude you, small seedless grapes could also be used, but the results won't be quite the same.

1 12-Ounce Package Extra Firm, Silken Tofu
½ Cup Olive Oil
1 Cup Granulated Sugar
2 Cups All-Purpose Flour
1 Cup Almond Meal

1½ Teaspoons Baking Powder
½ Teaspoon Baking Soda
¼ Teaspoon Salt
1 Teaspoon Vanilla Extract
¾ Teaspoon Almond Extract
¾ Cup Red Wine

1 Cup Champagne Grapes, Stemmed
½ Cup Pine Nuts
1 Tablespoon Turbinado Sugar (Optional)

Preheat your oven to 375°F and grease and flour a 10-inch springform pan.

In a large bowl, sift together the flour, almond meal baking powder, soda, and salt, stirring to make sure all of the ingredients are evenly distributed.

Using your food processor or blender, thoroughly purée the tofu, and blend in the oil and sugar until smooth. Pour the tofu mixture into your bowl of dry goods, followed by both extracts and the red wine. Stir just enough to combine, and don't fret over small lumps. Gently fold in the grapes and pine nuts, and pour the batter into your prepared pan and smooth out the top with your spatula. Sprinkle the top with the turbinado sugar, if desired.

Bake for 50–60 minutes until golden brown, and a toothpick inserted into the center comes out clean. Let cool for at least 15 minutes in the pan before unmolding.

SPICED ROSEMARY CHOCOLATE CHIP COOKIES

Makes 12–18
Large Cookies

They're certainly not your grandma's or your mom's chocolate chip cookies, but as a grown up twist on the classic, have far greater flavor complexity to offer. An unexpected hint of herbaceous rosemary is a welcome change of pace, further enhanced by the natural nuttiness of crunchy toasted pecans. Warm spices lend a bright kick just as the taste of chocolate and pecans begin to fade, lingering just long enough to leave you craving the sensation all over again.

½ Cup Margarine, Melted
½ Cup Dark Brown Sugar, Firmly Packed
⅓ Cup Granulated Sugar
2 Tablespoons Maple Syrup
½ Teaspoon Vanilla Extract
1 ½ Cups All Purpose Flour
¾ Teaspoon Ground Cinnamon
¼ Teaspoon Cayenne Pepper

¼ Teaspoon Smoked Paprika
1 Tablespoon Fresh Rosemary (or 1 Teaspoon Dried),
    Finely Chopped or Ground
½ Teaspoon Baking Soda
¼ Teaspoon Salt
1 Cup Toasted and Chopped Pecans
½ Cup (4 Ounces) Semi-Sweet Chocolate Chips or
    Chunks

Preheat your oven to 325 degrees and line two baking sheets with parchment paper or silpats. Set aside.

In the bowl of your stand mixer, blend together the melted margarine, both sugars, maple syrup, and vanilla until smooth and fully combined.

Sift the flour into a separate bowl, and add in all of the spices, rosemary, baking soda, and salt. Lightly toss both the pecan pieces and chocolate chips in, to coat with the flour.

Add the dry goods into the stand mixer in two additions, being careful not to overwork the dough but mix it just enough to bring everything together, without any pockets of flour lurking at the bottom. Be sure to scrape down the sides of the bowl between additions so that everything gets incorporated.

Scoop out dough with a medium-sized cookie scoop, or two large spoons in about 3 – 4 tablespoon portions. Give the cookies plenty of space on your prepared baking sheets, leaving at least an inch between blobs. I usually bake only 9 per sheet, to ensure that none of them spread and collide. Flatten the raw cookie dough out lightly with the palm of your hand, so that they're nice and round, and about ½ inch in thickness.

Bake for 12 – 16 minutes, watching closely to make sure that they are just barely golden brown around the edges when you pull them from the oven. They should still look fairly under-baked in the center, to ensure a soft and chewy texture.

Let cool on the sheets for 5 minutes, and then move them off to a wire rack. Store in an airtight container at room temperature for up to a week, if they last that long.

WINTER

ALMOND CHOCOLATE THUMBPRINT COOKIES

Yields Approximately 32 cookies

One cookie that I remember being a favorite on many holiday cookie platters was something called a "peanut butter blossom." Little more than a peanut butter cookie with a chocolate drop stuck in the center, it appealed to youngsters and those of mature palates alike. When baking for a celiac friend, however, I was at a bit of a loss—how to keep the integrity of this treat while still making it without gluten, and perhaps with a bit of renewed interest? The result was a cookie simply oozing with almond flavor that seems to melt in your mouth, along with the crunchy chocolate topper. If you can't get nonpareils, you can easily make your own (recipe page 235), but if those sprinkle-covered confections just don't appeal, you could make these like thumbprint cookies and fill the indents with chocolate ganache instead.

½ Cup Non-Dairy Margarine
⅔ Cup Smooth Almond Butter
½ Cup Granulated Sugar
½ Cup Dark Brown Sugar, Packed

1 Cup Almond Meal
1 Cup Garbanzo or Defatted Soy Flour
1 Teaspoon Baking Soda

½ Teaspoon Salt
¼ Teaspoon Almond Extract
1 Teaspoon Vanilla Extract

Enough Vegan Nonpareils to add one per cookie (approximately 32).

Preheat your oven to 375 degrees and line two baking sheets with a Silpat or parchment paper.

Toss the margarine and both sugars into your stand mixer, and cream thoroughly. Be sure to scrape down the sides before adding in the almond butter, and mix again to combine. Once the mixture is smooth and homogeneous, add in the almond meal, soy flour, baking soda, and salt all together and slowly mix it in. Finally, incorporate the vanilla.

Use your hands to shape the dough into balls the size of walnuts (about 1 inch in diameter) and place them each about an inch or so apart on the prepared baking sheets. Move the dough balls into the oven and bake for just 8 minutes before removing them and gently pressing a nonpareil into the center of each. Bake again for just 2 more minutes, and let the cookies cool on the sheets.

BLACK BLEEDING HEARTS

Makes 2 servings

Although I tend to be something of a hopeless romantic, Valentine's Day often brings out the worst in me. All the forced affection, cheap gifts, and downright appalling cards—I can't help but become a bit cynical about this awkward holiday. Straying from the cutesy candies and truffles, I would much prefer to cater to the disillusioned and serve something a bit more subversive. Jet-black hearts hemorrhaging rich chocolate blood? Pass the fork, please!

½ Cup Dutch-Processed Cocoa
   Powder
1 Tablespoon Black Cocoa Powder
⅓ Cup All-Purpose Flour
⅛ Teaspoon Baking Powder

2 Tablespoons Non-Dairy Margarine
⅓ Cup Granulated Sugar
6 Tablespoons Plain Soy or Coconut
   Creamer
½ Teaspoon Instant Coffee Granules

¼ Teaspoon Salt
½ Teaspoon Vanilla Extract

Preheat your oven to 425°F and lightly grease 2 4-ounce ramekins (preferably heart shaped, but plain round ones work just as well too).

Sift together both cocoa powders, flour, and baking powder into a medium bowl and set aside.

Place the margarine in a microwave-safe dish and heat it for a minute or so, just until melted. Stir in the sugar, soy creamer, coffee powder, salt, and vanilla. Slowly add in the dry ingredients and mix until just combined. Divide the batter evenly between your prepared ramekins, and place them both on a baking sheet so that they're easier to insert and remove from the oven. Bake for approximately 10 minutes, until the tops have set but they still wobble a bit when prodded. (The toothpick test wouldn't work here because you want a moist center.) Let cool for 10 minutes before serving.

BLACK PEARL TRUFFLES

*Makes about
2 dozen
truffles*

Wasabi, ginger, and black sesame join forces to create the sweet trinity known as "black pearl." High-quality dark chocolate works beautifully to both temper and accentuate the spices, and a light coat of crunchy sesame adds a touch of nutty relief. An Asian-inspired truffle for more adventurous eaters, it's certainly not the same old tired bonbon. Heat up your holiday gifts with a couple of these confections!

9 Ounces Bittersweet Chocolate,
    Chopped
¼ Cup Plain Non-Dairy Milk

¼ Cup Maple Syrup
1 Teaspoon Vanilla Extract
1¼ Teaspoons Ground Ginger

1 Teaspoon Wasabi Powder
¼ Cup Black Sesame Seeds

Place the chocolate, non-dairy milk, and maple syrup in a microwave-proof bowl, and heat for 1 minute. Even if it doesn't seem to have melted, give it a stir before giving it another 30 seconds. Repeat this until you can stir the mostly melted chocolate into a completely smooth mixture that has no lumps. Add the vanilla, ginger, and wasabi, and stir well to combine.

Lightly grease a 9 × 13–inch pan and pour the chocolate mixture into it. No need to spread it, just cover the pan with plastic wrap and refrigerate for an hour or two, until the mixture is the consistency of a thick ganache.

Using either a small ice cream scoop or melon baller, scoop small balls of the chocolate out and place them onto a Silpat-lined baking sheet. Portion out all of your truffle centers before proceeding, because things will get really messy from here on in. Next, you'll want to roll each scoop into a nicely round ball between the palms of your hands. The heat from your hands will start to melt the truffles, so work as fast as possible, but don't expect to finish this task without covering yourself in chocolate! Let the shaped truffles sit in the refrigerator for about 30 minutes to firm up again before rolling them in the black sesame seeds, ensuring that they're thoroughly covered.

BLOOD ORANGE UPSIDE DOWN CAKE

Serves 8–10

Blood oranges are such a beautiful, shocking crimson hue when first sliced open; I could hardly waste that beauty by merely extracting the juice and letting it get lost in some cake batter. Instead, by placing blanched slices of the citrus fruit at the bottom of a cake pan and inverting the whole thing once baked, you get not only a flavorful cake but an aesthetically pleasing one as well. Any sort of citrus would be a fantastic substitute too, but bear in mind that you'll need more lemons and fewer grapefruits to cover the surface of the cake.

2 Medium Blood Oranges
¼ Cup Non-Dairy Margarine
⅔ Dark Brown Sugar, Packed
½ Cup Unsweetened Apple Sauce

½ Cup Plain Non-Dairy Milk
1 Teaspoon Apple Cider Vinegar
⅓ Cup Canola Oil
½ Teaspoon Vanilla Extract

¾ Cup Granulated Sugar
2 Cups All-Purpose Flour
1½ Teaspoons Baking Powder
¼ Teaspoon Salt

First things first, thoroughly wash and dry your oranges. Break out your mandoline if you have one, or simply use a very sharp knife to cut the oranges into thin slices, about 4 mm thick each. Remove any troublesome pips, and place them in a medium saucepan and fill it with water so that the slices are covered, being gentle so as not to tear the membrane of your citrus. Bring the water to a boil, and then drain it away. Fill the pot back up with water and repeat this process twice more, in order to remove the bitterness from the orange, since the whole thing will be going into your cake.

Preheat your oven to 350°F and grease a 10-inch round cake pan.

Melt down the margarine and stir in the brown sugar, heating once more if necessary so that the sugar has dissolved. Pour into your prepared pan and place the oranges onto the sugar syrup, overlapping so that the bottom of the pan is completely covered, and set aside.

Now it's time to make the cake batter. Combine the apple sauce, non-dairy milk, and vinegar first; stir well; and allow the mixture to sit for 5 minutes. Add in the oil, vanilla, and sugar, and mix until homogeneous. Sift in the flour, baking powder, and salt last, and mix just until the dry goods are incorporated, and not a moment longer. Pour the batter carefully over the oranges, taking care not to disturb them. Smooth out the top with a spatula, and send it to the oven.

Bake for 30–40 minutes, until golden brown all over and a toothpick comes out clean—just make sure you don't poke all the way down to the bottom, because the caramel sauce should stay wet! Let the cake cool for 5 minutes before inverting the pan, revealing the oranges and caramel. Slice with a sharp knife to keep the pattern intact.

CHAI-SPICED POMEGRANATE PEARS

Serves 4

Poached pears are an easy and elegant dessert to serve after a rich meal, since they won't weigh you down quite like a slice of cake or pie. If you're serving a crowd, you can easily scale the recipe up two or three times without any trouble—just make sure you use a large-enough pot that it won't boil over on to the stove. This version takes advantage of pomegranate juice's naturally crimson hue to create a stunningly colored dessert, in addition to featuring its tart and tangy flavor. Accented by bright spices, it's both invigorating and comfortingly easy to eat.

Pomegranate Poached Pears:
4 Slightly Firm but Ripe Pears
¾ Cup Granulated Sugar
3 Cups 100 percent Pomegranate
　　Juice, No Sugar Added
1 Teaspoon Lemon Juice
4 Sticks Cinnamon

3 Star Anise
1 Inch Fresh Ginger, Grated
24 Black Peppercorns
16 Whole Cloves
½ Teaspoon Ground Cardamom
½ Teaspoon Vanilla Paste or Extract

Five-Minute Chocolate Sauce:
½ Cup Non-Dairy Milk
½ Cup Brown Rice Syrup
6 Ounces Semi-Sweet Chocolate,
　　Finely Chopped

Pomegranate Arils, to Garnish
　　(Optional)

Begin by peeling and coring the pears. My favorite way to remove the core is by turning the pears over and gently digging through the bottom with a melon baller. This way, you still have a perfectly shaped and intact pear, but no nasty seeds in the center.

Combine all of the remaining ingredients for the pears in a medium-sized pot and bring it to a boil. Carefully lower the pears into the water, cover, and turn the heat down to medium low, or a bare simmer. After 15–20 minutes, the pears should be fork-tender and soft to the touch. Turn off the heat but let the fruit continue to sit submerged for an additional 10 minutes to soak in as much flavor as possible. Serve warm with chocolate sauce, or cover and chill them and serve as a cold refreshing finale. Garnish with pomegranate arils if desired.

To make the chocolate sauce, simply combine the nondairy milk with the rice syrup in a medium saucepan and set over moderate heat. Bring the mixture just to a boil and then turn off the heat. Add in the chopped chocolate, stir to make sure that it's all submerged, and then let sit for 10 minutes so that it can melt. Stir vigorously until the sauce is completely smooth, and all of the chocolate chunks have entirely melted. Serve right away while still warm, or transfer to an airtight jar and store in the fridge. When you're ready to use it, reheat gently in the microwave for 30–60 seconds and stir thoroughly.

Note: Since the poaching liquid is so flavorful, I really can't bring myself to pour it down the drain. Instead, I like to strain out the whole spices, cool it down in the refrigerator, and then freeze it into a sorbet or granita. To do so, either pour the mixture into your ice cream maker as you would for any other sorbet, or fill a large shallow baking dish with it for a granita. Take the dish out every hour or so and scrape down the ice crystals until completely frozen. Voila, two desserts in one!

CHESTNUT MUFFINS

Makes 12 muffins

Inspired by the bag of chestnut flour I discovered at a specialty grocery store, I decided to take the opportunity to really highlight this starchy nut, since it's typically ignored by most home bakers. It needn't be in some fancy dessert, either—these muffins are most certainly basic breakfast fare, but so delicious they could easily be eaten any time of the day. If you can't get your hands on it, you can use finely ground almond flour instead of the chestnut flour . . . but of course, it won't be quite the same.

⅓ Cup Maple Syrup
½ Cup Canola Oil
6 Ounces Unsweetened Soy or
    Coconut Yogurt
1 Teaspoon Apple Cider Vinegar

½ Teaspoon Vanilla Extract
1 Cup Chestnut Flour
1 Cup Whole Wheat Pastry Flour, or
    White Whole Wheat Flour
1 Teaspoon Baking Soda

¼ Teaspoon Ground Cinnamon
¼ Teaspoon Salt
1 Cup Shelled and Roasted
    Chestnuts, Chopped
Turbinado Sugar

Preheat the oven to 350°F and either lightly grease 12 muffin tins or line them with papers.

Whisk together the agave, oil, soy yogurt, vinegar, and vanilla in a large bowl until fully combined. Add in both flours, baking soda, cinnamon, and salt, stirring until mostly smooth, but a few lumps are just fine. Make sure there are no remaining pockets of dry ingredients before folding in the chestnuts with a wide spatula.

Equally divide the batter among your prepared tins, filling each one nearly to the top, and sprinkle each one with just a pinch of turbinado sugar, if desired. Bake for 18–22 minutes until a toothpick inserted into the center comes out clean. Let the muffins cool in the pans for 10 minutes before transferring them to a wire rack to finish cooling.

CHOCOLATE CHESTNUT TORTE

Serves 10–12

It's very rare that we make a fire in the fireplace—which is often occupied by bowling pins rather than firewood—but when we actually do, we always use the heat from the smoldering cinders to roast chestnuts at the end of the day. The smoke imparts such an incredible flavor, unrivaled by other cooking methods, it's hard not to simply eat them out of hand. However, my favorite pastry application for them when I can restrain myself is this mousse, very simple in preparation and ingredients, but perfect for a fan of creamy, cool desserts. Smoothed on top of a dense chocolate cake, the two flavors and textures provide enough delicious contrast to keep you coming back for just one more bite.

Chocolate Torte:
3 Ounces Semisweet Chocolate, Finely Chopped, or about ½ Cup Semisweet Chocolate Chips
2 Tablespoons Canola Oil
1 12-Ounce Package Extra Firm Silken Tofu
1 Cup Almond Meal
⅓ Cup Chestnut Flour

⅓ Cup Dutch-Processed Cocoa Powder
¼ Cup Granulated Sugar
½ Teaspoon Baking Powder
¼ Teaspoon Salt

Chestnut Mousse:
8 Ounces Roasted Chestnuts*

1¼ Cups Plain Non-Dairy Milk, Divided
⅓ Cup Maple Syrup
½ Teaspoon Ground Cinnamon
¼ Teaspoon Vanilla Extract
Pinch Ground Cloves
1 Teaspoon Agar-agar Powder, or 1 Tablespoon Flakes, Ground

Preheat your oven to 325°F and lightly grease a 9-inch round springform pan to bake the torte base.

Combine the chocolate and oil in a microwave-safe dish and heat in the microwave for 30 seconds at a time, stirring thoroughly at each interval, until completely melted and smooth. Set aside and let cool for 5 minutes.

Thoroughly drain the tofu and place it in your food processor or blender. Purée, pausing to scrape down the sides of the work bowl with your spatula, until smooth. Add in the melted chocolate and blend until everything is fully incorporated and there are no streaks of chocolate or tofu remaining.

Into the machine, add the almond meal, chestnut flour, cocoa, sugar, and salt. This is a gluten-free batter, so you don't need to be concerned about overmixing, but don't overdo it. Pulse until the batter comes together smoothly, with no pockets of unmixed ingredients hiding anywhere. Run your spatula through the mixture just to check and make sure.

Continued on next page

Pour the very thick batter into your prepared springform and smooth out the top with your spatula. Tap the pan gently on the counter a few times to remove air bubbles that may be trapped. Bake for 25–30 minutes, until the top is dry to the touch and slightly crackled. Let cool completely before topping with the mousse.

Moving on to the chestnut mousse, first, place the shelled chestnuts in your (clean!) food processor or blender, and purée thoroughly. I find that I can get a smoother mixture if the chestnuts are still hot, but it will still work out just fine if they have already cooled. Just be patient and allow the machine to work out all of the lumps. With the motor running, stream in ½ cup of the soymilk, and maple syrup. Sprinkle the cinnamon, vanilla, and cloves over the top, and pulse to incorporate. Set aside.

Set a medium saucepan over moderate heat and vigorously whisk together the agar and remaining soymilk, making sure that there are no lumps. Heat the two together until boiling rapidly, whisking the whole time, and immediately pour into the chestnut mixture while the motor runs. Make sure it blends to an entirely silky-smooth consistency, because any agar that isn't incorporated will solidify into unpleasant chunks. Quickly pour the mousse onto your baked chocolate torte and smooth it down evenly over the top. If you'd like, use your spatula to leave decorative swirls in the mousse.

Allow the mousse to cool to room temperature before moving the springform into your fridge. Let cool for at least for about 3 hours, or until thoroughly chilled and the mousse has set. Slice and serve with chocolate sauce, if desired.

*To roast your chestnuts, start with approximately 1 pound in the shell. You're likely to have some extra, but since it will be hard to avoid snacking on at least a handful, that should work out in your favor. Cut x's into the flat side of each chestnut and place them all on a large square or rectangle of aluminum foil. Wrap them up in a little foil package and place either on the embers of a recently extinguished fire (in the fireplace or fire pit, not on the stove, I hope!) or a 400°F preheated oven.

Roast for 20–40 minutes, checking periodically, until the x's seem to open up a bit and they become easy to peel. The time can vary greatly depending on the heat source and freshness of your chestnuts, so be sure to keep an eye on them at all times. Remove all shells before cooking with or eating them.

FIVE-SPICE SNAPS

**Makes about
1½ dozen
cookies**

These cookies will wake you up and out of that dreary winter feeling! Bringing a bit more heat with Chinese five-spice powder, it's about time spice cookies had some real bite to them. Even I was amazed at the rave reviews these unassuming crackled cookies garnered, and I still can't plan on having a single morsel leftover just one day after making a single batch. Do yourself a favor and double the recipe, or keep your cookies well hidden!

These cookies are an ideal treat for celebrating the Chinese New Year in February.

½ Cup Non-Dairy Margarine
⅔ Cup Granulated Sugar
2 Tablespoons Molasses
1½ Cups All-Purpose Flour

2 Teaspoons Five-Spice Powder
   (page 224)
1 Teaspoon Baking Soda
⅛ Teaspoon Salt

1 Tablespoon Water
¼ Cup Turbinado Sugar

Preheat your oven to 350ºF degrees and line a baking sheet with parchment paper or a Silpat.

Install the paddle attachment on your stand mixer and place the margarine in the bowl first, beating it briefly on low speed. This will soften it up a bit and make it easier to incorporate the dry goods. Add in the sugar and molasses, and cream thoroughly, pausing to scrape down the side of the bowl as necessary. The mixture should be grainy but otherwise smooth, without any ribbons of unmixed molasses remaining.

In a separate bowl, lightly whisk together the flour, five-spice powder, baking soda, and salt to combine. Add this flour mix into your stand mixer, followed by the water, and let the mixer do its thing. Be patient; it may take a few minutes for the dough to come together.

Pinch off 1–2 tablespoons' worth of dough at a time, roll them into smooth balls in the palms of your hands, and then roll them each around in the turbinado sugar. Place the cookies spaced about 1 inch apart on your prepared baking sheet, and press down lightly to flatten out the tops. If the dough starts sticking to your hands, just lightly moisten them with cool water.

Bake the cookies for 8 to 12 minutes, and let cool on sheets. If you prefer chewier cookies, bake for a shorter time; for crunchier, bake for longer. Let the cookies rest on the sheets for about 10 minutes before transferring them to wire rack to finish cooling.

GRAPEFRUIT GEMS

Makes 12–16 bars

Lemon bars are a favorite cookie at every bake sale, potluck, or dessert buffet I've been to. It's hard to improve on such a classic, but throw a little grapefruit in, and you'll get an entirely new sweet sensation. Of course, if you chose to stick to the prototypical lemon bar and substitute lemon juice concentrate instead of the grapefruit, well, I wouldn't protest.

Crust:
1 Cup Oat Flour
½ Cup Confectioner's Sugar
2 Tablespoons Cornstarch
3 Tablespoons Non-Dairy Margarine, Melted
2–3 Tablespoons Non-Dairy Milk

Grapefruit Topping:
1 Cup Instant Mashed Potato Flakes
¾ Cup Unsweetened Grapefruit Juice Concentrate
1 Cup Granulated Sugar
3 Tablespoons Cornstarch
1 Tablespoon Non-Dairy Margarine

Preheat your oven to 350°F and line an 8 × 8–inch square pan with parchment paper cut to size, lightly greasing and flouring it once fitted in the pan.

To make the crust, sift together the oat flour, sugar, and cornstarch into a large bowl to combine. Drizzle in the melted margarine and 2 tablespoons of soymilk, and mix thoroughly until homogeneous. If it's still too dry to come together, add 1 last tablespoon of soymilk. Press the mixture into your prepared pan using slightly moistened palms or the bottom of a flat measuring cup, making sure it's an even layer. Bake for 10–15 minutes until browned around the edges. Remove from the oven, reducing the heat to 325°F, and chill the crust for at least 30 minutes.

Meanwhile, combine the mashed potato flakes and grapefruit concentrate in a microwave-safe bowl and heat for 1–2 minutes, until the liquid has been absorbed. Move the contents of the bowl into your food processor or blender, and thoroughly purée until the mixture is entirely smooth. Combine the sugar and cornstarch before adding both in at the same time, and pulse to combine. Drop the margarine in and pulse a few more times; there should still be enough residual heat to melt it.

Pour the grapefruit filling on top of the cooled crust, tapping the pan on the counter a few times and smoothing out the top with a spatula, and bake for about 20 minutes. It may not look entirely set when done, but the edges will seem slightly firm and just barely browned. Let cool completely and chill in the fridge before removing the bars, using the parchment paper as a sling, and cut into rectangles.

GREEN TEA AND GRAPEFRUIT CUPCAKES

Makes 12 cupcakes

Sharing the same sort of bright, intense, almost-bitter characteristics, green tea and grapefruit have synergistic properties that are seldom utilized. Definitely a more sophisticated balance of flavors, these cupcakes are for mature, adventurous palates.

Candied Peels:
1 Grapefruit
1 Cup Granulated Sugar, Divided
½ Cup Water

Green Tea Cupcakes:
1 Cup Plain Non-Dairy Milk
1 Teaspoon Apple Cider Vinegar
¼ Cup Canola Oil

6 Tablespoons Granulated Sugar
1 Teaspoon Vanilla Extract
1½ Cups All-Purpose Flour
2 Teaspoons Matcha Powder
1 Teaspoon Baking Powder
½ Teaspoon Baking Soda
¼ Teaspoon Salt
¼ Teaspoon Ground Ginger

Grapefruit Frosting:
1 Cup Vegetable Shortening
3 Cup Confectioner's Sugar
1–3 Tablespoons Grapefruit Juice
Zest of 1 Grapefruit

First candy the grapefruit peel. Use a paring knife to remove all of the peel and pith from the grapefruit. Slice the peel into smaller strips, and then toss them all into a pot of hot water. Bring this to a boil, and then drain. Fill the pot back up with fresh water, and repeat this process two more times. Be sure to completely drain out the bitter water each time. Now add in ¾ cup of the sugar and the final ½ cup of water. Stir until the sugar has dissolved and cook until it reaches 230°F according to your candy thermometer. Use a slotted spoon to remove the peels from the pot, letting the excess syrup drip off, and place them on a Silpat or piece of parchment, making sure that none are overlapping. Reserve the syrup and let cool. The peels will be tacky, so toss them in the remaining sugar to make them easier to store and handle.

For the cupcakes, preheat your oven to 350°F and line 12 standard muffin tins with cupcake papers.

Combine the non-dairy milk and vinegar, and allow about 5 minutes for the "milk" to curdle. Pour it into a large bowl, and add in the oil, sugar, and vanilla. Whisk thoroughly until somewhat frothy, and set aside. In a separate bowl, sift together the flour, matcha, baking powder and soda, salt, and ginger. Stir well and add to the main bowl. Stir just enough to combine, and divide the batter equally between your prepared tins. Bake for 15–20 minutes, until a toothpick inserted into the center comes out clean. While still warm, brush the excess syrup over the tops of the cupcakes. You probably won't use it all, but just make sure that each cupcake is nicely moistened.

To make the frosting, simply mix together the shortening, sugar, and zest in your stand mixer, starting at a low speed. When the sugar is mostly incorporated, add in 1 tablespoon of juice. Turn up the speed to high and whip for 2 minutes; if the frosting is too stiff, add in more juice until it reaches your desired consistency. Continue to beat for 2 or 3 more minutes, until light and fluffy. Frost cupcakes as desired and top each with one strip of candied grapefruit peel.

IRISH CRÈME SQUARES

*Makes 12–16
squares*

Whenever St. Patrick's Day struck on a school day in my elementary years, I distinctly remember that we would be served green bagels and green milk to celebrate, as if that were at all festive or even minimally appetizing. Not eager to go that route again, I'd much prefer to borrow inspiration from a sweet drink, Irish Cream, and turn it into a rich bar cookie. How's that for Irish spirit?

Almond Crust:
1½ Cups Almond Meal
½ Cup All-Purpose Flour
¼ Cup Confectioner's Sugar
2 Tablespoons Natural Cocoa Powder

¼ Cup Non-Dairy Margarine or
  Coconut Oil, Melted

Irish Crème Topping:
1 Cup Vegan "Sour Cream"
½ Cup Granulated Sugar

1½ Teaspoons Instant Coffee
  Granules
2 Tablespoons Whiskey
2 Tablespoons All-Purpose Flour
1 Teaspoon Vanilla Extract
¼ Teaspoon Almond Extract

Preheat your oven to 350°F.

In medium bowl, mix the almond meal, flour, sugar, and cocoa to combine. Pour in the melted margarine and stir to moisten all of the crumbs. Press this mixture into an ungreased 8 × 8–inch square pan, and bake for 10 minutes.

For the filling, start by whisking the "sour cream" and sugar together. Dissolve the coffee granules in the whisky before adding both into the bowl, along with the flour, vanilla, and almond extract. Mix well to thoroughly incorporate everything, but take care not to whisk too much air into the mixture. Pour this over the crust and bake for 14–16 minutes until filling is set, much like a cheesecake. It will still seem wobbly when you jiggle the pan, but it will continue to firm up as it cools. After letting the pan cool to room temperature, chill for at least 2 hours before cutting into squares.

JEWELED POMEGRANATE COOKIES

Makes about 2 dozen cookies

The best thing about icebox cookies is that you can make the dough days or even weeks in advance, stash it in your freezer until a need arises, and then just slice off as many cookies as you'd like. Perfect for feeding unexpected guests or sending off as gifts, this version is speckled with ruby red pomegranate arils for a pleasantly tart bite and subtle crunch. Always a crowd-pleaser, it's also very versatile if you'd like to substitute any other sorts of dried fruits or nuts.

¾ Cup Non-Dairy Margarine
1 Cup Confectioner's Sugar
1½ Cups All-Purpose Flour

½ Teaspoon Ground Ginger
¼ Teaspoon Salt

¾ Cup Pomegranate Arils, Fresh or Dried
1 Teaspoon Vanilla Extract

Preheat your oven to 350°F and lightly grease a mini muffin pan.

Using your stand mixer, cream together the margarine and sugar until thoroughly combined into a homogeneous paste. In a separate bowl, sift the flour and mix in the ginger and salt. Add the pomegranate arils into the dry mixture, tossing to coat. Add these dry ingredients into your stand mixer slowly, in 2 additions. Incorporate the vanilla, and although the dough will still seem very dry, you won't need to add any more liquid. Just be patient and keep mixing it until everything comes together into a cohesive ball of dough.

Pinch off 1–2 tablespoons of dough at a time, roll into a ball between your palms, and place into one indentation in your prepared mini muffin pan. Use your fingertips to press the dough out flat, to evenly fill the bottom. Repeat until the pan is full. This allows you to skip the traditional step of chilling the dough, and still get a lovely smooth round shape.

Bake for 15–18 minutes until golden colored around the edges but still seemingly soft in the center. If you wait until they're entirely brown, the outsides are likely to burn or become quite hard. After letting them sit in the pan for 10 minutes, move the cookies onto a wire rack to finish cooling. Let the pan cool before regreasing and refilling with more dough if needed.

LEMON-LIME MADELEINES

Makes 12 madeleines

Made famous by the French writer Proust and loved for centuries, madeleines may sound complicated but are truly nothing more than little cakes. Deriving their delicate scalloped shape from special pans, they're sure to impress with little effort on your part. However, even if you don't have madeleine pans, that doesn't mean that you can't enjoy these dainty tea cakes too. You can also make them by greasing and flouring oven-safe soup spoons and balancing them on the rim of a baking sheet. Only fill them with about 1–2 teaspoons of batter, and be very careful not to knock them over when moving the pan about. Bake for only 10–15 minutes since they're smaller and will therefore cook much faster.

1 Cup All-Purpose Flour
2 Tablespoons Tapioca Flour
⅓ Cup Granulated Sugar
1 Teaspoon Baking Powder

¼ Teaspoon Salt
¼ Cup Non-Dairy Margarine, Melted
¼ Cup Plain Non-dairy Milk
¼ Cup Lime Juice

1 Tablespoon Lemon Zest
½ Teaspoon Vanilla Extract

Preheat your oven to 400°F and lightly grease and flour a standard madeleine mold.

In a medium bowl, mix together both flours, sugar, baking powder, and salt, stirring well to ensure that all of the ingredients are evenly distributed. Separately, combine the melted margarine, non-dairy milk, and lemon juice, quickly whisking together and pouring them into the dry goods. If you wait too long, the non-dairy milk will curdle, and you'll end up with a grainy batter, so don't just stand around, get mixing! Once the batter is mostly smooth, toss in the lemon zest and vanilla extract, stirring just enough to thoroughly incorporate everything.

Spoon about 2–3 tablespoons of batter into each indentation so that they're about ⅔ of the way full. Pop the pan into the oven and immediately reduce the temperature to 375°F. Bake for 16–20 until they've puffed up a bit and are nicely browned around the edges. The tops will be much lighter in color, so don't use their appearance as an indication of doneness. You can also use the toothpick test if you're unsure.

MAPLE CORN MUFFINS

Makes 12

My favorite way to eat cornbread is with a generous drizzle of pure maple syrup over the top, soaking in and saturating the already-moist crumb, but that can sure get messy. It was only a matter of time before the two became fused together in one perfect package—a sweet, hearty muffin that simply begs to be toasted and slathered with a buttery spread.

1 Tablespoon Non-Dairy Margarine
    or Coconut Oil
2 Cups Corn Kernels, Canned,
    Fresh or Frozen, Thawed and/or
    Washed
2 Cups White Whole Wheat Flour

1 Cup White or Yellow Corn Meal,
    Finely Ground
2½ Teaspoons Baking Powder
½ Teaspoon Baking Soda
½ Teaspoon Salt
Pinch Freshly Ground Black Pepper

2 Tablespoons Flaxseeds, Ground
1 Cup Maple Syrup
1¼ Cups Plain Non-Dairy Milk
1½ Teaspoons Apple Cider Vinegar
¼ Cup Olive Oil

Preheat your oven to 400°F and lightly grease 12 muffin tins.

Set a medium skillet over moderate heat and melt the margarine or coconut oil. Pat your corn kernels dry and toss them into the hot skillet. Stirring occasionally, cook for about 15–20 minutes until the corn is evenly toasted and golden brown. Remove from the heat and let cool while you assemble the rest of the muffin batter.

Combine the flour, cornmeal, baking powder, baking soda, salt, and flaxseeds together in a large bowl so that it's a homogeneous mix, and set aside. In a separate bowl, whisk together the maple syrup, "milk", lemon juice, and olive oil. Pour the wet ingredients into the dry, and stir just until combined. Remember, it's better to have a few lumps than an overmixed tough batter! Add your corn and use a large spatula to fold the kernels in gently. Distribute the batter between your prepared cups and move them into the oven. Bake for 10 minutes before turning down the temperature to 375 degrees, without opening the door. Bake for 10–15 additional minutes, until a toothpick inserted into the center comes out dry. Cool on a wire rack.

MAPLE-PECAN LAYER CAKE WITH GINGERBREAD FROSTING

Makes 14–18 servings

For every holiday dinner, the task of creating one showstopping grand finale of a dessert falls on me, and it seems as though the cakes get bigger and taller with each passing year. This is one behemoth of a baked good that is guaranteed to draw oohs and ahs from any crowd: three layers of maple cake studded with copious amounts of toasted pecans, smothered in a spicy gingerbread frosting and crowned with even more pecans. Definitely a luxurious number that only comes out once a year at most, it's a dessert that you're sure to remember better (and more fondly) than that itchy sweater you got from Aunt Sally.

Maple-Pecan Cake:
4 Cups All-Purpose Flour
½ Cup Almond Meal
¼ Cup Granulated Sugar
1 Tablespoon Baking Powder
1½ Teaspoons Baking Soda
¾ Teaspoon Salt
½ Cup Canola Oil
1½ Cups Plain Non-Dairy Milk
1½ Cups Maple Syrup
½ Cup Unsweetened Apple Sauce

1 Tablespoon Apple Cider Vinegar
1 Teaspoon Vanilla Extract
1½ Cups Chopped Pecans, Toasted

Gingerbread Frosting:
1½ Cups Non-Dairy Margarine
4½ Cups Confectioner's Sugar
2 Tablespoons Molasses
1 Teaspoon Vanilla Extract
1½ Teaspoons Ground Cinnamon
1½ Teaspoons Ground Ginger

¼ Teaspoon Ground Cloves
¼ Teaspoon Ground All Spice
¼ Teaspoon Ground Nutmeg
1–3 Tablespoons Plain Non-Dairy
   Milk

⅓–⅔ Cup Chopped Pecans, Toasted
Whole Pecans, For Decoration
   (Optional)

Preheat your oven to 350°F; lightly grease and flour either three 8-inch round or two 9-inch round cake pans.

In a large bowl, sift together the flour, almond meal, sugar, baking powder and soda, and salt, making sure that all of the dry goods are evenly distributed throughout the mix. Set aside.

Separately, mix together the nondairy milk, maple syrup, apple sauce, vinegar, and vanilla. Allow the mixture to sit for about 5 minutes so that the "milk" just begins to curdle. Don't worry if you don't see any dramatic changes though.

Pour the liquid ingredients into the bowl of dry, followed by the pecan pieces. Use a large spatula to bring the two together, stirring just enough to create a smooth batter. Divide the batter evenly between your prepared pans and tap them each a few times on the counter to smooth out the tops and knock out air bubbles.

Bake the cake rounds for 25–30 minutes, until lightly browned all over and a toothpick inserted into the centers comes out clean and dry. Let cool completely before turning the cake layers out of the pans and frosting.

When you're ready to make the frosting, begin by placing the margarine in your stand mixer, and beat briefly with the whisk attachment just to soften. Add in the sugar, molasses, vanilla, all of the spices, and 1 tablespoon of the soymilk. Start the mixer back up on the lowest speed setting so that the sugar doesn't splatter out onto the kitchen walls. Once mostly incorporated, pause to scrape down the sides of the bowl, and then turn it up to high. If it seems too thick and dry, add more "milk," 1 tablespoon at a time, until it reaches your desired consistency. Whip for a full 5 minutes until light and fluffy.

To assemble the cake, spread a healthy dollop of frosting on the bottom cake layer, and once smoothed out evenly, sprinkle with ⅓-cup chopped pecans. Repeat with the following layer if using three, and then cover the whole tower with more frosting. Decorate with a border of whole pecans around the top, if desired.

MARZIPAN TEA CAKE

Serves 8–10

Although you're more likely to see marzipan sculpted into the shape of fruits and cute woodland animals this time of year, I value it more as an ingredient than as a modeling medium. Chopped up and baked into this tender loaf, it becomes so soft that the pieces practically melt in your mouth, the aroma of almonds infused through every last crumb. Soaked in your choice of spirits, this cake does actually get better with age, so feel free to make it up to one week in advance.

2 Tablespoons Non-Dairy Margarine, Melted

2 Tablespoons Canola Oil

½ Cup Dark Brown Sugar, Packed

⅓ Cup Granulated Sugar

⅔ Cup Plain Non-Dairy Milk

⅓ Cup Orange Juice

1 Teaspoon Apple Cider Vinegar

2 Cups All-Purpose Flour

⅔ Cup Almond Meal

1 Teaspoon Baking Powder

½ Teaspoon Baking Soda

½ Teaspoon Salt

4 Ounces Marzipan (page 239)

½ Teaspoon Vanilla Extract

¼ Teaspoon Almond Extract

¼ Cup Amaretto or Rum (Optional)

Preheat your oven to 350°F and lightly grease and flour an 8 × 4–inch loaf pan.

First, in a medium bowl, whisk together the melted margarine, oil, both sugars, nondairy milk, orange juice, and vinegar, until thoroughly combined. Let sit for about 5 minutes for the "milk" to curdle, making it similar to buttermilk. This will help give your cake a better rise and also keep the crumb a bit moister.

In a separate bowl, mix together the flour, almond meal, baking powder and soda, and salt. Chop up the marzipan into small, raisin-sized cubes and toss them into the bowl until they're evenly coated with flour. It's important to make sure that the pieces aren't sticking together, or else you may end up with big clumps of marzipan baked onto the bottom of your loaf. You may want to go through the mixture lightly with your hands to pull apart any clumps.

Pour your mixture of wet ingredients into the bowl of dry, followed by both extracts. Using a wide spatula, fold the two together, stirring as few times as possible, until the batter is mostly smooth. Pour the batter into your prepared loaf pan and smooth out the top lightly with your spatula. Bake for 40–50 minutes, until golden brown on top and a toothpick inserted into the center of the cake comes out clean. While still hot out of the oven, pour the amaretto or rum all over the top, if using, so it can soak in and redistribute throughout the cake nicely. Let cool in the pan.

Best if aged for 1 to 7 days at room temperature, wrapped tightly in plastic.

MERINGUE KISSES

Makes approximately 4 dozen cookies

Easily my most sought-after recipe, I can't begin to count the number of requests I've received pleading for me to spill my meringue-making secrets. At long last, here's the truth, for the whole world to see. There really is no secret, and my meringues are actually stunningly easy to make. Unlike egg-white-based meringues, these aren't nearly as finicky in humid weather, and they're almost impossible to overwhip.

Traditionally, I tend to think of meringue kisses as a holiday treat, because that's when my mom would pull out the stained recipe card written by her nana and start egg whites whipping in the stand mixer. Our favorite version was always replete with either a generous infusion of cocoa powder or a smattering of miniature chocolate chips. I've provided the method for a basic vanilla variety, leaving you with a blank canvas with which to paint in any flavor you desire. Just be careful not to add too many additional extracts or flavored oils, because the meringues will become increasingly unstable with added fats.

⅓ Cup Ener-G Egg Replacer
¾ Cup Water

½ Cup Granulated Sugar
1 Teaspoon Vanilla Extract

Preheat your oven to 300°F and line two baking sheets with Silpats or parchment paper.

Combine the egg replacer with the water in your stand mixer and turn it up to the highest setting, whipping the mixture for a full 5 minutes. At that time, begin to sprinkle in the sugar slowly, and proceed to whip for 5 more minutes. It will have substantially increased in volume at this point, making for a light and fluffy concoction, much like whipped cream. Scrape down the sides of the bowl, remove any excess batter on the beater, and gently fold in the vanilla extract with a wide spatula.

Drop dollops of your fluff on baking sheet, each about the size of a golf ball. You don't need to leave a whole lot of space between cookies because they shouldn't spread, but make sure they still have some room to breathe. Bake for 30–35 minutes until they no longer look shiny—you do not want them to brown. If anything, the cookies should only show a very light golden color on the bottom, but I would certainly not push them any further than that. Turn off oven but leave meringues in until the oven shuts itself off in order to further dry the cookies to a crispy texture. Once finished, store in airtight container at room temperature, for up to a week.

MINT CHOCOLATE MACARONS

Makes 60 macaron shells, 30 macaron cookies

Distinctly different from the coconut macaroons that most Americans know, this French invention has taken the world by storm, and now few can escape the siren song of this ephemerally light, crispy sandwich cookie. Traditionally built upon ground almonds and whipped egg whites, it's hard to even consider the possibility of a vegan version, but one bite of this knockout combination of refreshing mint and light cocoa crunch will convince any naysayer. Endless flavor adaptations are possible, but I gravitate toward this festive combo for a guaranteed holiday hit.

If you do wish to experiment with other flavor combinations, be careful not to tweak the basic structure, because this is one very finicky baked good. Measurements must be as precise as possible; I don't recommend beginning bakers to start their kitchen odyssey here. Be prepared to experience a batch or two of less-than-perfect shells at first, because it takes some practice and experience to know when the batter is just right. Your patience and persistence will be rewarded, however—there's simply nothing else quite like these treats.

Cocoa Macaron Shells:

3 Tablespoons Ener-G Egg Replacer
½ Cup Water
¼ Cup Granulated Sugar
2 Cups Minus 2 Tablespoons
    Confectioner's Sugar
1 Cup Finely Ground, Blanched
    Almond Meal

2 Tablespoons Natural Cocoa Powder
1½ Teaspoons Chocolate Extract

Vanilla-Mint Filling:
1 Cup Non-Dairy Margarine
3 Cups Confectioner's Sugar
½ Teaspoon Matcha (Optional, For
    Color)

2 Tablespoons Plain Non-Dairy Milk
1 Teaspoon Peppermint Extract
1 Whole Vanilla Bean

First, place the Ener-G and water in a microwave-safe dish and whisk thoroughly to combine. Once the mixture is lump free, microwave for 30 seconds. Let stand for 2 minutes or so before transferring to your stand mixer.

Install the wire whisk attachment and whip the mixture for 3 minutes to build up a basic but fairly tight foam before slowly sprinkling in the granulated sugar, a teaspoon or two at a time. Beat for a total of 7–8 minutes, until you achieve a fluffy, glossy meringue with firm peaks.

In a food processor, combine the confectioner's sugar, almond meal, and cocoa, and pulse to thoroughly mix and break up any small lumps or coarse pieces of almonds. Do not allow the machine to get warm, or overprocess this mixture, because you don't want the almonds to turn into butter. Sift the resulting powder mixture in a fine mesh sieve before proceeding. Don't be tempted to skip this step; it's critical to ensure a smooth macaron shell and prevent any bigger pieces of almonds from slipping in.

Add the almond mixture into your meringue, along with the chocolate extract, and very gently fold it in. Mix with care so as not to beat the tar out of it and pop all of the bubbles you've worked so hard to create. The batter should still be fluffy but somewhat sticky, and flow like hot lava in thick ribbons.

Transfer the batter to a piping bag fitted with a medium-sized round tip, and pipe out fairly flat rounds of about 1 inch in diameter on pieces of ungreased parchment paper. Allow about an inch of space between each macaron shell. Use just barely moistened fingers to tap down any irregular peaks on top of the shells so that they're completely smooth domes.

Let the macaron shells sit at room temperature for about 1½ hours so that they form a very slight "skin" and don't blow out in the oven. Once properly aged, preheat your oven to 300°F, carefully slide the parchment papers onto baking sheets, and bake for 9–11 minutes, depending on their size. They should not brown at all, but should be dry to the touch and have slight but noticeable "feet" on the bottoms.

Slide the parchment papers from the hot baking sheets and let the macaron shells cool completely before attempting to remove them from the paper.

Meanwhile, you can prepare the filling to sandwich them with. Simply place the margarine in your stand mixer with the whisk attachment in place, and beat briefly to soften. Add in the confectioner's sugar and matcha if using, and start the machine on low speed, until the sugar is mostly incorporated and is no longer in danger of flying out of the bowl. Scrape down the sides of the bowl and add in the nondairy milk and mint extract. Turn up the mixer to high speed and whip for about 5 minutes, until the filling/frosting is light and fluffy. Split your vanilla bean in half and scrape out the insides with the side of your knife. Add the seeds in to the mix, scrape down the sides of the bowl once more to ensure that all ingredients are thoroughly combined, and beat for 1 more minute.

Transfer to a piping bag and apply the filling to the flat side of one macaron shell. Sandwich with a second shell and repeat until all of the cookies are used.

PEPPERMINT MOCHA TRIFLE

Serves 15–20

As the holidays creep onto my radar, a strange shift in flavor preferences occurs: All of a sudden, I simply can't get enough of anything with peppermint. Throw in some chocolate and I'm in heaven. Keep going and give the whole thing a hint of coffee, and watch out—it's a dangerously addictive combination! This recipe is great for a crowd.

Coffee Cake:
1½ Cups Strong Brewed Coffee, Cooled
½ Cup Plain Non-Dairy Milk
1 Teaspoon Apple Cider Vinegar
2 Teaspoons Instant Coffee Granules
1 Teaspoon Vanilla Extract
½ Cup Canola Oil
1 ⅓ Cup Granulated Sugar
2 Cups All-Purpose Flour

1 Cup Whole Wheat Pastry Flour
1½ Teaspoons Baking Powder
¾ Teaspoon Baking Soda
½ Teaspoon Salt
¼ Teaspoon Ground Cinnamon

Mint Chocolate Custard:
2 12-Ounce Packages Extra Firm Silken Tofu
⅔ Cup Granulated Sugar

1 Teaspoon Vanilla Extract
½ Teaspoon Peppermint Extract
10 Ounces Semisweet Chocolate, Finely Chopped
1 Cup Plain Non-Dairy Milk
12 Standard-Sized Candy Canes, Crushed
¾ Cup Mini Chocolate Chips, or Chopped Semisweet Chocolate

Preheat your oven to 350ºF and lightly grease a 13 × 9-inch baking dish.

In a large bowl, whisk together the coffee, soymilk, vinegar, coffee granules, vanilla, oil, and sugar. Whisk to dissolve the coffee granules and set aside. Take out a second bowl and sift both flours into it, along with the baking powder and soda, salt, and cinnamon. Stir to distribute the dry goods throughout, and then pour the wet ingredients on top of the dry. Mix until just combined, ignoring any stray lumps to prevent overmixing, and pour the batter into your prepared pan. Smooth down the top with your spatula, and bake for 28–34 minutes, until a toothpick comes out of the center clean.

Meanwhile, pull out your food processor or blender to get started on the custard. Drain out as much excess liquid from the tofu as possible, and then thoroughly purée both until entirely smooth. Add in the sugar, vanilla, and peppermint extract, and pulse to combine. Place the chopped chocolate and soymilk in a microwave-safe dish, and heat for 1–2 minutes, stirring well after each minute, until the chocolate has melted and the mixture is smooth. Pour the chocolate into the tofu mixture and purée for another minute, scraping down the sides as needed to ensure that the custard is homogeneous. Transfer to a bowl, cover with plastic wrap, and chill. It will become thicker as it sits in the fridge.

When your cake is baked and cooled, cut it into small cubes. Arrange some of the cubes on the bottom of a 2-quart trifle dish into one even layer, and then spread a layer of the chocolate custard on top. Sprinkle a handful of the crushed candy canes and chocolate on top. Repeat this process until all components have been used up.

PERSONAL PANETTONES

Makes 12–18 panettones

Asweet bread that originated in Italy and is typically enjoyed during the holiday season, panettones are large cylindrical loaves that generally weigh 2 or 3 pounds. Unless you're feeding an army, this amount of fruit-studded bread is doomed to be left over and forgotten. But by making a smaller batch, and individual servings, you get both fresher miniloaves and a more personalized treat.

⅓ Cup Dried Currants
⅓ Cup Dried Cranberries
⅓ Cup Dried Cherries
⅓ Cup Rum
1 Cup Plain Non-Dairy Milk
1¼-Ounce Package Active Dry Yeast

⅓ Cup Granulated Sugar
5 Tablespoons Canola Oil or
    Margarine, Melted
½ Teaspoon Salt
1 Tablespoon Flaxseeds
2 Tablespoons Water

¼ Teaspoon Anise Extract (Optional)
½ Teaspoon Almond Extract
1 Teaspoon Lemon Zest
1 Teaspoon Orange Zest
2 Tablespoons Sliced Almonds
3–4 Cups All-Purpose Flour

In a microwave-safe bowl, combine all of the dried fruits with the rum and heat on high for just a minute, until the liquid has been mostly absorbed by the fruit. Set aside.

Heat the "milk" for 1 minute just until warm. Sprinkle the yeast over it and let it sit for 10–15 minutes, until the yeast is frothing away happily. Pour this into your stand mixer, along with the sugar, oil, and salt.

Use a coffee or spice grinder to blitz the flaxseeds into a fine powder, and then add in the water and pulse a few times to combine. Pour the flax mixture into the bowl, followed by the anise extract (if using), almond extract, both zests, sliced almonds, and those boozy currants that you set aside earlier. Add in any excess rum as well. Mix briefly to distribute the ingredients, and install your dough hook attachment.

Start with 3 cups of the flour and mix it in on low speed. If the resulting dough seems very soft and sticky, add up to one more cup of flour, until it is merely tacky, but will hold together in a ball. Let the stand mixer knead your dough for 10 minutes, or do this step by hand on a lightly floured surface for 15 minutes. Once smooth and elastic, drop your dough ball into a greased bowl, turn it once to coat, and cover with plastic wrap. Let it sit in a warm spot for about an hour and a half until doubled in volume. After that time has elapsed, punch the dough down and cut the dough into 12 pieces if using popover pans, or 18 if using standard muffin tins. Roll each piece in your hands until nicely rounded and even, and place them into lightly greased pans of your choice. Let them sit again for 1 hour, and as they near the end of their final rise, you can begin heating your oven to 350°F.

Bake the panettones for 20–25 minutes, until the tops are nicely browned and they smell irresistible.

PISTACHIO NOG

Yields about 2 cups

There are a few brands of "soy nog" that pop onto the market when the season rolls around, but this homemade version blows all those thin, weak brews clear out of the water. Super creamy, rich, and only boozy if you want it to be, you may find it hard to stop making it even after the winter holidays have passed.

½ Cup Roasted, Unsalted Pistachios, Soaked Overnight
1½ Cups Water

¼ Cup Light Agave Nectar
¼ Teaspoon Ground Nutmeg
Tiny Pinch Black Salt

$^1/_{16}$ Teaspoon Xanthan Gum (Optional)
Freshly Grated Nutmeg

Thoroughly rinse and drain the soaked pistachios, and then toss them into your food processor or blender. For this recipe, a high-speed blender is recommended, but you can still make this nog without; the results just may not be quite as creamy.

Start on a low speed, and once the nuts are mostly broken down, crank it up to high, and thoroughly purée for at least 3–4 minutes, until it appears completely smooth. If the mixture still seems gritty, you may want to pass it through a strainer, depending on how capable your machine is.

Add in the agave, nutmeg, and salt, and blend on high for another minute. Taste and adjust seasonings if needed. Refrigerate until chilled before enjoying, or up to 5 days.

To serve, mix with rum as desired and top each cup with an additional pinch of fresh nutmeg.

Note: Have leftover nog after the guests have all gone home? Give it a whirl in your ice cream maker for an instant frozen treat! Still have a bunch of friends and family to feed the morning after? Simply soak a couple slices of crusty bread in it for a few minutes and panfry it to make decadent French toast.

POMEGRANATE GRANOLA

Makes about 10–12 servings

For reasons unknown to me, one of the most frequent search terms that brought new readers to my blog was pomegranate granola. I had never heard of pomegranate granola before, much less provided a recipe for it, but it certainly sounded like a great idea. So for all of those searchers who left disappointed, here's what you've been looking for! Pumped full of antioxidants and that tart-and-sweet pomegranate flavor, it was definitely a great suggestion.

3 Cups Rolled Oats
1 Cup Almond Meal
¼ Cup Flaxseeds, Ground
1 Cup Chopped Walnuts
1 Cup Pistachios
¼ Cup Olive Oil

¾ Cup 100 percent Pomegranate Juice
¼ Cup Pomegranate Molasses
½ Cup Dark Brown Sugar, Firmly Packed
½ Teaspoon Salt

½ Teaspoon Ground Cinnamon
¼ Teaspoon Ground Ginger
1 Cup Dried Pomegranate Arils

Preheat your oven at 300°F.

Toss together the oats, almond meal, ground flaxseeds, and nuts in a large bowl. In a separate bowl, whisk the oil, pomegranate juice and molasses, sugar, salt, and spices to combine. Pour the wet ingredients into the dry mixture and stir to thoroughly moisten every last crumb.

Spread the mixture on a large ungreased jelly roll pan, smoothing it into as thin a layer as possible with little overlap. After about 15 minutes, the top should begin turning golden brown, at which time you should remove the pan and stir the mixture. This will expose the uncooked bits of granola and begin to separate it into clumps. Return it to the oven and bake for another 15 minutes before stirring again. Bake for another 15 minutes if the mixture is still too pale and moist, until the granola is a uniform golden brown and mostly dry. In total, it will take about 30–45 minutes to bake. Cool completely before mixing in the dried pomegranate and storing in an airtight container at room temperature.

TRIPLE CITRUS CUPCAKES

Makes 24 cupcakes

Suffering from the midwinter blahs, when it seems that not a single fresh fruit remains in the grocery store, and there's nothing but kale and potatoes thriving in the harsh frozen tundra outside? Reach for citrus—and don't stop at just one type! By combining three different zesty flavors into one cupcake, you'll get a brighter, well-rounded flavor that's sure to shake off that gloomy, grey feeling.

Although I didn't bother to write down this recipe when I first made it, expecting it to be nothing special, it received such rave reviews that I was practically forced right back into the kitchen to re-create it! We even sell it for special orders at the restaurant I work at now. It's always such a hit, I tend to make fairly large batches, but you can halve the recipe to get an even dozen.

Orange Cupcakes:
2 Cups Orange Juice
1–2 Tablespoons Orange Zest
½ Cup Canola Oil
2 Teaspoons Vanilla Extract
2⅓ Cups All-Purpose Flour
1½ Cups Granulated Sugar
⅓ Cup Potato Starch
2 Teaspoon Baking Powder

1 Teaspoon Baking Soda
½ Teaspoon Salt

Lemon Curd Filling:
1½ Cups Granulated Sugar
9 Grams Agar-agar Powder
2½ Cups Lemon Juice
Zest of 1 Lemon

Lime Frosting:
1 Cup Non-Dairy Margarine
3 Cups Confectioner's Sugar
2 Tablespoons Non-Dairy Milk
½ Teaspoon Vanilla Extract
Zest of 1 Lime

Preheat your oven to 350°F and line 24 standard muffin tins with cupcake papers. Set aside.

In a large bowl, whisk together the orange juice, zest, oil, and vanilla. In a separate bowl, combine the flour, potato starch, sugar, baking powder, baking soda, and salt, until all of the dry goods are well distributed. Pour the liquid ingredients into the bowl of dry and whisk just until the two come together in a smooth batter—a few lumps are just fine, and much better than overmixing and creating tough cupcakes.

Distribute the batter evenly between your prepared tins and bake for 15–20 minutes, until a toothpick inserted into the center of the cakes comes out dry. Let cool completely before filling or frosting.

Meanwhile, to make the lemon curd filling, whisk together the sugar and agar powder to combine. Place the two into a medium saucepan along with the lemon juice and zest and turn on the stove to medium heat. Whisk to break up any lumps of sugar and continue whisking occasionally as it comes up to temperature. Once the mixture comes to a boil, turn off the heat and transfer the still-liquid curd to a heat-safe container. Allow it to come to room temperature before refrigerating until you're ready to use it. This step is very important, because tossing it in the fridge too early will weaken the gel, and you will end up with a runny filling.

Finally, the frosting comes together very simply, starting with softening the margarine in your stand mixer. Slowly incorporate the confectioner's sugar, adding it incrementally with the mixer on a low speed, to make sure it doesn't fly out and onto the kitchen walls. Add in the nondairy milk, zest, and vanilla last, and then gradually increase the speed up to high, scraping down the sides of the bowl as needed to ensure that everything is incorporated. Whip until light and fluffy, approximately 5 minutes.

To assemble your cupcakes, take a paring knife and carve a small cone out of the center of each cupcake. Discard, eat, or save the centers to turn into cake truffles (page 216). Give your set lemon curd a good stir to loosen it slightly, and then add a spoonful to the now-empty indent of the cupcake. Carefully top with frosting as desired, being sure to fully cover the filling.

TRIPLE GINGER CHEESECAKE

Makes 12–14 servings

Ginger lovers, rejoice! There has never been a better time to celebrate this spicy root, and no better dish in which to feature it. Providing a kick in three luscious layers, a mere sliver of this piquant cheesecake will get your mouth buzzing.

Spiced Crust:
1¾ Cups Vanilla Wafer Crumbs (page 243)
½ Teaspoon Ground Cinnamon
½ Teaspoon Salt
3 Tablespoons Non-Dairy Margarine or Coconut Oil, Melted
1 Tablespoon Molasses
1 Tablespoon Plain Non-dairy Milk

Ginger Filling:
1 12-Ounce Package Extra Firm Silken Tofu
2 8-Ounce Containers Vegan "Cream Cheese"
3 Inches Fresh Ginger, Finely Grated
1 Cup Granulated Sugar
1 Teaspoon Vanilla Extract

Vanilla Topping:
1½ Cups Vegan "Sour Cream," or Puréed Silken Tofu
⅓ Cup Granulated Sugar
2 Teaspoons Vanilla Extract
1 Teaspoon Ground Ginger

Preheat your oven to 350°F and lightly grease a 9-inch springform pan.

Toss together the vanilla wafer crumbs, cinnamon, and salt to combine. Mix the melted margarine, molasses, and soymilk in a small dish, and drizzle all of these wet ingredients over the crumb mixture. Stir thoroughly to moisten all of the crumbs and press into your prepared pan. Bake for just 10 minutes until no longer shiny. Let cool and lower the oven temperature to 325°F.

For the filling, take out your food processor or blender and toss in the tofu. Purée thoroughly, scraping down the sides of the bowl as needed, until completely smooth. Add in the "cream cheese," grated ginger, sugar, and vanilla, and pulse to incorporate. Pour the filling on top of the crust, tap gently on the counter to remove any air bubbles, and smooth down the top with a spatula. Bake for 45–50 minutes until the sides pull away from the pan slightly.

Meanwhile, prepare the topping. Simply combine all ingredients and whisk until smooth. When the main cake is ready, pour over the top, smooth with a spatula, and bake for an additional 8–10 minutes until softly set.

Let cool to room temperature before stashing in the fridge for at least 3 hours until thoroughly chilled.

WARMING LEMON RISOTTO

Serves 2-3

Take rice pudding and give it a bit of Italian flare, and you might come close to this comforting dish. Creamy but still somewhat toothsome, with a satisfying crunch of toasted almonds every now and then, this is the rice pudding to win over self-proclaimed detractors. Take advantage of the fresh citrus so abundant now, but make it into something hot to keep you warm during these cold months. It also makes for a sweet and unique breakfast option!

¾ Cups Plain Non-Dairy Milk

1 Cup Water

2 Chamomile-Mint Tea Bags

1 Tablespoons Olive Oil

½ Cup Arborio Rice

Zest of 1 Lemon

⅓ Cup Granulated Sugar

½ Teaspoon Vanilla Paste or Extract

Pinch Salt

¼ Cup Whole Toasted Almonds

Begin by mixing together the non-dairy milk and water in a small saucepan and heat the mixture just to a boil. Add in your tea bags after turning off the heat, cover the pan, and let steep for 15–20 minutes. After your liquids have darkened in color from the tea, give it a taste and decide if it has enough flavor for you. If not, let the bags steep longer or even add in another one. Once the tea has reached your desired strength, squeeze out the tea bags.

In a separate medium saucepan over medium-low heat, toss together the oil and rice so that all the grains are evenly coated. Let this cook for 3 or 4 minutes, just until the rice begins to appear translucent. At that time, pour in about a third of your liquid. No need to be precise, just make sure you end up incorporating the liquid in a total of three additions. Stir the rice as it cooks to coax out the starch and enhance the overall creaminess until most of the moisture has been absorbed. Add in half of the remaining soy mixture and repeat until you have used up all of the liquid and the rice is soft, slightly toothsome, and creamy much like rice pudding. Turn off the heat and add in the lemon zest, sugar, vanilla, salt, and almonds. Serve warm.

You can make this ahead of time and heat it back up to serve, but I would suggest leaving the almonds out until the last minute if you plan to do so, just to prevent them from getting soggy.

CHAI-SPICED PISTACHIO BRITTLE

*Makes about
1 ¹/₄ pounds*

Peanut brittle is always a huge hit around my family, but for one fateful holiday season, I thought it might be fun to spice things up a bit. Alluring green pistachios are perfectly accented by the symphony of warm seasonings typically found in a glass of chai tea. It ended up becoming one of my most sought-after and frequently requested recipes, still attracting new admirers to this day.

1 Cup Granulated Sugar
½ Cup Light Corn Syrup
¼ Cup Water
¼ Teaspoon Salt
1 ½ Cups Pistachios
1 Teaspoon Baking Soda
1 Teaspoon Ground Ginger
¾ Teaspoon Ground Cinnamon

½ Teaspoon Ground Cardamom
¼ Teaspoon Ground Cloves
¼ Teaspoon Ground Nutmeg
Pinch Freshly Ground Black Pepper
½ Teaspoon Vanilla Extract
1 Tablespoon Margarine

Before beginning these candies, lay out a silpat or piece of parchment paper close to the stove, in preparation for the finished brittle. Set aside.

Place the sugar, corn syrup, water, and salt in a medium sauce pan over moderate heat. Stir gently to combine, and cook until the sugar has dissolved. From this point on, do not stir the mixture anymore, or else you may end up with large, ugly sugar crystals. Insert your candy thermometer, and let the hot sugar cook and bubble away until it reaches 300 degrees, otherwise known as the hard crack stage.

Meanwhile, combine the pistachios, all of the spices, and baking soda in a medium bowl. Once the sugar reaches the proper temperature, add these dry ingredients in, and stir like mad! Remove the pan from the heat, and quickly stir in the vanilla and margarine as well, continuing to mix vigorously until the margarine has melted. Pour the liquid candy out onto your prepared silpat or parchment paper, and use a spatula to spread and flatten it out as much as possible.

Let rest undisturbed until completely cool, and snap into pieces as desired.

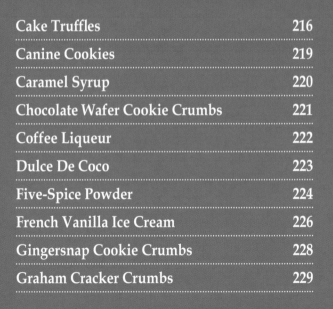

COMPONENTS AND ACCOMPANIMENTS

CAKE TRUFFLES

Nothing goes to waste in my kitchen! Taught to save scrupulously and appreciate even the tiniest bits and pieces that may be left over, it would be a crying shame to let something as delicious as cake end up in the trash. Though you could always just snack on those scraps without further adornment, with just a tiny bit of extra effort, you can create a whole new dessert instead. This recipe is so easily adaptable, you can combine any number of flavors to create unique pairings every time. There are no exact measurements, because it all depends on how much cake you have on hand. Just trust your instinct and be prepared to get your hands dirty!

Cake Scraps, Any Flavor

Leftover Frosting, Any Flavor

Semisweet Chocolate, Melted and Tempered

Toss all of your scraps into a large bowl and use your fingers to break them up into coarse crumbs. Add in a dollop of frosting and gently but thoroughly massage it into the cake. Continue to add spoonfuls of frosting as needed, until all of the crumbs are thoroughly moistened and can be pressed together into a cohesive sort of "dough."

Pinch off walnut-sized balls of cake and frosting and roll them between your palms until smooth. Place each ball on a baking sheet lined with parchment paper or a Silpat, continuing to form balls until all of the cake mixture is used. Move the sheet of truffle centers into the fridge and let chill for at least an hour.

Once the truffle centers are chilled, place a good amount of chocolate in a microwave-safe dish. You'll want more than you think you'll need to cover all of the truffles so that you have a good depth of melted chocolate to dip in and fully cover them. Microwave the chocolate for a minute and stir thoroughly. Continue to heat at intervals of 30 seconds, stirring well between each round, until the chocolate is fully melted and smooth.

Drop one truffle at a time into the chocolate, make sure it's fully submerged, and use a fork to lift it up from beneath; do not stab it! Gently tap the truffle on the edge of the chocolate bowl to allow the excess chocolate to drip off, and return it to the baking sheet. Repeat with the remaining cake balls. Let the truffles stand in a cool place until the chocolate has solidified. Store the finished cake truffles in an airtight container either in a cool dark area or in the fridge.

CANINE COOKIES

With so many enticing aromas and tempting treats coming out of the kitchen, let's not forget that our furry friends want in on the action too! My dog, Isis, has grown pickier with age, but even the pickiest pooch could hardly turn up her nose at a soft banana and oat cookie, complete with tempting carob morsels.

When baking for your furry friends, just remember to steer clear of nondigestible items that could make them sick, such as chocolate, raisins, onions, avocado, macadamia nuts, mushrooms, persimmons, unbaked yeast dough, and spices.

1 Ripe, Medium-Sized Banana
¼ Cup Canola Oil
¼ Cup Warm Water

1 Cup Whole Wheat Flour
1 Cup Rolled Oats
2 Tablespoons Flaxseeds, Ground

⅓ Cup Malt-Sweetened or
Unsweetened Carob Chips

Preheat your oven to 350°F and line a baking sheet with either parchment paper or a Silpat.

This recipe is so uncomplicated that I'm betting that you could figure out the procedure even without written instructions. Just in case you'd like some guidance, however, here's how it goes: Mash the banana and mix it with the oil and water. Add the flour, oats, ground flaxseeds, and carob chips, and stir thoroughly to combine. This will create a rather stiff dough, so you may want to use your hands to lightly knead and press it together into a cohesive ball.

Turn it out onto a lightly floured surface and roll it out lightly to about ½ inch in thickness. Use cookie cutters to make any shapes you desire, and move the cookies to your prepared baking sheet. Bake them for about 20–25 minutes, until dry to the touch. Make sure they're completely cool before sharing them with your pup!

Store in an airtight container, but be aware that these have more moisture than typical dog biscuits, so they won't last for nearly as long—2 weeks at room temperature, max. For extended storage, toss them into the freezer and thaw as needed.

CARAMEL SYRUP

Makes 2 cups

Thinner than a caramel sauce and not quite as rich or creamy, whisk this syrup into hot coffee, or use to make caramel frosting.

2 Cups Granulated Sugar
1¼ Cups Hot Water, Divided

In a medium saucepan with tall sides, combine the sugar and ½ cup of the water, stirring with a rubber spatula until all of the sugar is moistened. Turn on the heat to medium, and from this point forward, do not stir the mixture; instead, gently swirl the pan to mix. This will prevent the mixture from crystallizing prematurely.

Cook the sugar, swirling occasionally, until it turns deep amber in color, but do not allow it to begin smoking or smelling burnt. You want to cook it to a fairly dark shade to give it the most flavor, but if it smells burnt, it's already too late and you must start again. Once it begins to color, it will progress very quickly, so do not walk away at this point.

Once deeply colored, very carefully pour in the remaining hot water. The mixture is likely to sputter and bubble up, so you may want to stand to the side while making this addition, and it doesn't hurt to have long sleeves to cover your arms, just in case. The mixture may seize and crystallize a bit on the bottom of the pan, but don't worry, it's easy to fix. Continue to cook the syrup over gentle heat until any crystals are dissolved and the mixture is completely smooth again.

Let cool completely before using or storing in a glass jar.

CHOCOLATE WAFER COOKIE CRUMBS

Makes about 4 cups of crumbs

¼ Cup Non-Dairy Margarine
¼ Cup Vegetable Shortening
1 Cup Granulated Sugar
¼ Teaspoon Salt
1 Teaspoon Vanilla Extract

2 Cups All-Purpose Flour
¾ Cup Natural Cocoa Powder
¼ Teaspoon Baking Powder
¼–½ Cup Plain Non-Dairy Milk

Preheat your oven to 350°F and line two baking sheets with Silpats or parchment paper.

In your stand mixer, cream together the margarine, shortening, and sugar, until completely smooth and homogeneous. Add in the salt, vanilla, flour, cocoa, and baking powder, starting the mixer at a low speed so as not to toss the dry ingredients out. The mix will still seem very dry, so start by adding in ¼ cup of non-dairy milk, and let the mixer process that thoroughly. If it still is too dry to press together into a ball, continue to add 1 tablespoon of soymilk at a time while continuing to mix. When it's at the correct consistency, use your hands to form it into a ball, and then divide that in half. Lay each half out on one Silpat and lightly coat the tops with flour. Use a rolling pin to flatten the dough down to about ⅛ inch thick. Take a pizza roller and slice the dough vertically and horizontally at about 1-inch intervals. No need to be precise here, these cuts just help the dough to cook more evenly and become crisp all over.

Bake each sheet individually, for about 18–22 minutes, until no longer shiny and the edges feel solid. The cookies will continue to firm up and become more crisp as they cool, but if you find that some pieces are still soft, just pop them back into the oven for an additional 5 minutes or so.

Once both sheets are baked and cooled, break them up and give them a spin in your food processor to create even crumbs. Store at room temperature in an airtight container until ready to use.

COFFEE LIQUEUR

1½ Cups Granulated Sugar
2 Cups Freshly Brewed Coffee
2 Tablespoons Instant Coffee Granules

2 Cups Vodka
2 Teaspoons Vanilla Extract

In a medium saucepan, combine the sugar, coffee granules, and brewed coffee. Set over moderate heat, stirring occasionally, until all the granules and sugar have dissolved. Remove the pot from the heat and stir in the vodka and vanilla. Let cool completely and pour into a large bottle, seal tightly, and let sit in a dark place for at least 30 days before using. If it seems a bit cloudy at the bottom, shake vigorously prior to use.

DULCE DE COCO

1 13.5-Ounce Can Coconut Milk
1 Cup Dark Brown Sugar, Packed

¼ Teaspoon Salt
½ Teaspoon Vanilla Extract

Combine all ingredients except for the vanilla in a medium saucepan over medium-high heat. Once the mixture comes to a boil, reduce the heat to med-low, cover, and simmer for about 20 minutes. Remove the lid, turn heat down further to low, and simmer for approximately 35–40 more minutes, stirring occasionally, until thickened. Add in the vanilla and pour into a glass jar for storage, allowing it to cool completely before securing the lid.

FIVE-SPICE POWDER

A powerful mixture of anise, pepper, cinnamon, fennel seed, and cloves, we owe Chinese cuisine for this spicy representation of the five basic tastes: salty, sweet, sour, bitter, and savory. Ratios and exact blends vary depending on who you ask, and every cook seems to have their own family recipe, so go ahead and tweak until it pleases your palate. Most grocery stores will stock the seasoning in the spice aisle, but here's how I like to mix mine up at home.

2 Tablespoons Ground Star Anise

2 Tablespoons Crushed Cinnamon Stick Pieces

2 Teaspoons Ground Fennel Seeds

2 Teaspoons Crushed Szechuan Peppercorns

¼ Teaspoon Ground Cloves

Toss all of the spices into a coffee or spice grinder and just let the machine pulverize everything to a fine powder. Make sure that there are no large pieces or unmixed pockets of spice before transferring to an airtight jar. Dark-colored glass is the best option, because light will degrade the flavors faster.

If you can't find Szechuan peppercorns, an equal amount of either black or white peppercorns can be substituted for a slightly different but similarly fiery bite.

FRENCH VANILLA ICE CREAM

If you ask me, nothing complements a sweet grand finale like a simple scoop of vanilla ice cream, cutting the richness, providing good contrast, and still allowing the main dessert to shine through. Don't let that stop you from playing around with this classic, though. Consider it a base for every other flavor you might dream up. Go wild, add spices or extracts at will; steep coffee beans or fresh herbs in the soymilk; experiment with fruit purées to substitute part of the liquid. Dress it up or leave it as is; a solid vanilla ice cream is a must in my book!

2 Cups Plain Soymilk
¼ Cup Bird's Custard Powder*
½ Cup Granulated Sugar
Pinch Salt
2 Whole Vanilla Beans or 2 Tablespoons Vanilla Paste
3 Tablespoons Margarine or Coconut Oil

In a medium saucepan, whisk together the soymilk, custard powder, sugar, and salt while the liquid is still cold, being sure to get out any clumps. Use a knife to split the vanilla beans down the middle and scrape out the seeds. Toss the seeds and spent pods into the pan, or the vanilla paste, if using.

Set the mixture over medium heat, whisking continuously until it comes to a boil. Immediately turn off the heat and carefully remove the pods. Don't throw them out though; they can still be washed off, dried, and placed in a container of sugar to make vanilla sugar.

While the custard is still hot, whisk in the margarine and keep stirring until it has fully melted and incorporated. Let chill completely in the refrigerator before proceeding.

The custard will be very thick once chilled, so be sure to whisk vigorously, or give it a quick spin in the blender before churning in your ice cream maker according to the manufacturer's instructions.

Transfer the soft ice cream into an airtight container and let rest in the freezer for at least 3 hours before serving, until solid enough to scoop.

Note: Custard powder mimics the rich flavor that eggs would traditionally provide, giving it that extra creamy decadence so hard to come by in commercial vegan offerings. However, an equal amount of cornstarch will work as well if you can't get your hands on it.

GINGERSNAP COOKIE CRUMBS

Makes about 4 cups of crumbs

¼ Cup Vegetable Shortening
¼ Cup Non-Dairy Margarine
¼ Cup Granulated Sugar
½ Cup Molasses
2½ Cups All-Purpose Flour

¾ Teaspoon Ground Ginger
½ Teaspoon Ground Cinnamon
½ Teaspoon Salt
¼ Teaspoon Baking Powder

Preheat your oven to 350°F and line two baking sheets with Silpats or parchment paper.

In your stand mixer, cream together the margarine, shortening, and sugar, until completely smooth and homogeneous. Add in the molasses, flour, spices, salt, and baking powder, starting the mixer at a low speed so as not to toss the dry ingredients out. The mix will still seem very dry, so start by adding in ¼ cup of soymilk, and let the mixer process that thoroughly. Resist the temptation to add in more liquid— there should be plenty to bring this dough together, just as long as you're patient and let the mixer do its thing. Use your hands to form the dough into a ball, and then divide that in half. Lay each half out on one Silpat, and lightly coat the tops with flour. Use a rolling pin to flatten the dough down to about ⅛ inch thick. Take a pizza roller and slice the dough vertically and horizontally at about 1-inch intervals. No need to be precise here, these cuts just help the dough to cook more evenly and become crisp all over.

Bake each sheet individually, for about 10–16 minutes, until no longer shiny and the edges feel solid. The cookies will continue to firm up and become more crisp as they cool, but if you find that some pieces are still soft, just pop them back into the oven for an additional 5 minutes or so.

Once both sheets are baked and cooled, break then up and give them a spin in your food processor to create even crumbs. Store at room temperature in an airtight container until ready to use.

GRAHAM CRACKER CRUMBS

Makes about 2¼ cups crumbs

While I never have any trouble finding vegan graham crackers, I often get e-mails asking where I find them, what brand they are, and maybe could I ship a box or ten. Quite a lot of fuss for such a common pantry staple! Or so I thought. It was only when I decided to cut out crappy processed junk like high-fructose corn syrup did I realize the depth of the issue. The only choices were to purchase crackers with honey or the dreaded HFCS. Not one to compromise or surrender, the solution was actually easy: Make them myself! Easier than going through the trouble of rolling out sheets of crackers, this method cuts right to the chase, no finesse required. Perfect vegan graham cracker crumbs, coming right up!

1½ Cups Graham flour
½ Cup Dark Brown Sugar, Packed
¼ Teaspoon Baking Soda
¼ Teaspoon Salt

3 Tablespoons Canola Oil
1 Tablespoon Molasses
1 Teaspoon Vanilla Extract
4–5 Tablespoons Plain Non-Dairy Milk

Preheat your oven to 350ºF and lightly grease a sheet pan.

Toss everything together in a large bowl, adding the non-dairy milk last, 1 tablespoon at a time, until there are no dry patches in the dough and it sticks together a bit. Dump it out onto your prepared baking sheet and use your hands to spread it out as thinly as possible. It will help if you slightly moisten your hands, since the dough is a bit sticky. Bake for 10 minutes, at which point it should look somewhat puffy and just barely browned around the edges. Take a metal measuring cup or flat-bottomed glass and flatten the dough back out, pressing firmly so that it's all even. Return the sheet to the oven for about 5 more minutes. It will still be a bit floppy at this point, so let it cool for a few minutes before tearing it into small pieces and baking for a final 10–15 minutes, stirring every 5 minutes like you would for granola.

Let cool completely and then smash into crumbs by either placing the crumbs in a plastic bag and crushing it with a rolling pin or pulsing them briefly in your food processor. Store in an airtight container at room temperature.

INTENSE CHOCOLATE SORBET

Makes about 1 pint

You may think that a concoction without any nondairy milk or cream would be a bit lacking in flavor or texture, but you will be surprised at how rich and luscious this simple sorbet is. Even more decadent than full-fledged chocolate ice cream, this is a frozen treat for true chocoholics only!

2 Cups Warm Water, Divided
1 Cup Granulated Sugar
1 Cup Dutch-Processed Cocoa Powder

2 Ounces Dark Chocolate, Finely Chopped
1 Teaspoon Vanilla Extract
½ Teaspoon Salt

Combine ¼ cup of the water and all of the sugar in a medium saucepan over medium-high heat. Don't stir for the first couple of minutes, until the sugar dissolves and the mixture comes to a boil. Continue cooking, stirring occasionally, until the sugar becomes a golden caramel color after about 5–10 minutes. Add the remaining water carefully, standing back in case of splashing. The caramel will seize and sputter a bit, and don't worry if it appears to harden. Cook gently once again until the caramel is dissolved, immediately removing the pot from the heat once smooth. Thoroughly whisk in the cocoa powder, vanilla, and salt, making sure there are absolutely no lumps. Finally, add in the chocolate and whisk until fully melted and the mixture is smooth. Chill thoroughly before freezing in your ice cream maker per the manufacturer's instructions. Once churned, pack the sorbet into a container and freeze it solid before serving.

LADY FINGERS

**Makes about
2 dozen
ladyfingers**

½ Cup Granulated Sugar
2 Teaspoons Cornstarch
1 Cup Cake Flour
1 Teaspoon Baking Powder

½ Cup Plain Soy or Coconut Yogurt
½ Teaspoon Apple Cider Vinegar
½ Teaspoon Vanilla Extract
Confectioner's Sugar

Preheat your oven to 350°F and line two baking sheets with Silpats.

In a medium bowl, sift together the sugar, cornstarch, flour, and baking powder, mixing to evenly distribute all of the dry ingredients. In a separate dish, mix together the yogurt, vinegar, and vanilla. Pour the yogurt mixture into the dry goods and mix with a wide spatula. It will seem very dry at first, but trust me, you won't need any more liquid; just keep stirring until it comes together into a thick, rather stiff batter. Spoon the batter into a piping bag fitted with a large round tip (about ½ inch) and pipe 3-inch-long strips onto your prepared sheets, spacing each about 1 inch apart.

Sprinkle a light coat of confectioner's sugar over the cookies with a sifter or fine mesh strainer, and bake for 9–12 minutes, until the cookies no longer appear shiny and are just barely browned around the edges.

LEMON DROP JAM

Makes approximately 3 cups

Otherwise known in my kitchen as "sunshine in a bottle," this cheerful yellow spread was a last-ditch attempt to combat the winter blues. Though there were no fresh fruits to make jam from, I was determined to make something sweet to spread on toast, and hopefully lift my dampened spirits a bit. Seeking out the abundant citrus fruits, I wanted to try something a bit unusual, and this jam certainly is an uncommonly tasty treat! Infused with vanilla beans, it's intensely lemon-flavored, but perfectly balanced by the sugar so that it's not mouth-puckeringly sour. An easy way to add brightness and perk up select desserts or simply serve at breakfast, a few lovingly decorated jars of it can also make for fantastic holiday gifts.

12 Small Lemons
1 Cup Water
4 Cups Granulated Sugar

1 3-Ounce Pouch Liquid
    Pectin
1 Teaspoon Vanilla Paste

First, getting the most time-consuming part of this recipe out of the way, zest and juice all of the lemons; you should end up with about 1 ½ cups total of juice and zest. Pour both into a medium saucepan, along with the water and the sugar. It may seem like a whole lot of sugar, but remember, we're making jam here, and it would end up being unpleasantly tart and sour without it.

Over moderate heat, whisk the mixture occasionally until the sugar has dissolved and it reaches a rapid boil. Add the liquid pectin all at once and stir vigorously. If this addition has knocked down the heat, bring the mixture back to a boil, stirring all the while, and boil hard for approximately 30 seconds to "activate" the pectin. Turn off the heat and stir in the vanilla. Let the jam cool for about 5 minutes before pouring into glass jars and screwing on the lids. This will create a basic heat seal to preserve the jam slightly longer, but the jars should still be stored in the fridge once completely cooled. Refrigerated, the lemon jam should keep for about 1 month.

LIMONCELLO

Makes 8–9 cups

10 Meyer Lemons
1 750 ml Bottle Vodka

3½ Cups Water
2½ Cups Granulated Sugar

Peel each of the lemons, trimming away any white pith as that will contribute too much bitterness to the mix. Place the peels in a 2-quart jug or pitcher and squeeze in the juice from the lemons as well. Pour in the vodka and cover with lid, allowing the mixture to sit at room temperature for about a week.

In a saucepan over medium heat, combine the water and sugar, cooking for about 5 minutes until the sugar has completely dissolved. Cool to room temperature and add it into the container of lemons and vodka. Let the flavors meld, undisturbed, for another 2 days at minimum. The longer you let it sit, the more flavorful it will be, so try to remain patient!

When you want to use your limoncello, strain out the peels, transfer the liquid into smaller bottles if desired, and keep refrigerated.

NONPAREILS

Vegan nonpareils can be difficult to find in some areas, and if you don't want to go through the hassle of ordering them online, they're actually pretty easy to make yourself. Start by melting down a good amount of chocolate; the exact amount isn't important—just make sure you have enough that it won't burn while melting but not so much that you can't deal with it all before it begins to cool. Transfer the liquid chocolate into a piping bag fitted with a medium-sized round tip. Pipe out small dollops, each about the size of a nickel, onto a piece of parchment paper or a Silpat. While they're still warm, carefully pour sprinkles on top, covering each as thoroughly as possible. Let them cool completely to set, and then store in an airtight container at room temperature. Be careful though—these are just as much fun to eat plain as in a cookie, so hide them well!

PUMPKIN BUTTER

1 15-Ounce Can Pumpkin Purée
½ Cup Maple Syrup
2 Teaspoons Ground Cinnamon
1 Teaspoon Ground Ginger
½ Teaspoon Ground All Spice

¼ Teaspoon Ground Cloves
Pinch Ground Nutmeg
Pinch Black Pepper
Pinch Salt

In a small saucepan over medium-low heat, mix together the pumpkin mush and maple syrup until they're both fully combined. If you prefer your spread to be sweeter, don't be shy and feel free to add in as much syrup as it takes to satisfy that sweet tooth. This is one recipe that can be modified with great ease, and still remains pretty much infallible.

Continue to stir the pumpkin slowly for about 10–15 minutes, or until the mixture has thickened to the point that it's a consistency similar to very thick oatmeal or polenta. It's very important to keep stirring, so don't walk away! If you do, your pumpkin may scorch and burn onto the bottom of the pan, and there's simply no going back once you've reached that stage.

Once thickened, take your pan off the heat and mix in all the spices and salt.

Take a clean empty jar and spoon in the hot pumpkin butter. Allow it to cool before topping it off with the lid, and then make sure it's reached room temperature before moving it to the fridge. Refrigerated, it should last about a solid month—that is, if it isn't all eaten before then.

SHORTCUT MARZIPAN

**Makes about
2 cups**

Typically made through a laborious, drawn-out process involving skinning almonds, boiling sugar syrup to a specific temperature, and kneading hot almond paste until your hands are raw, it's no surprise that marzipan is rarely made at home these days. Unfortunately, many commercial varieties are now made with egg whites, which leaves few options for vegan bakers. Fear not, there is still an alternative to the pain and suffering! Though it's a bit softer than standard marzipan, my quick method yields a pleasingly workable sculpting material and baking ingredient—not to mention, it is way tastier and about a hundred times fresher than what's been sitting around on grocery store shelves for months on end.

2 Cups Raw, Blanched, and Slivered
    Almonds
⅔ Cup Light Agave Nectar

¼ Teaspoon Rose Water or Orange
    Blossom Water (Optional)
¼ Teaspoon Almond Extract

Pinch Salt

Although a high-speed blender will definitely do a better job on this recipe, you can still use a regular food processor just fine as well. The results will simply be slightly less smooth.

Place the slivered almonds in your blender or food processor and grind them down into as fine a powder as possible without actually turning them into almond butter. If the machine begins to get hot, take a break and let it rest until it cools so that the almonds don't release all of their oil and have it separate out. You're good to go when it looks like flour, or just slightly coarser.

In a microwave-safe dish, heat the agave for about 1 minute to warm and loosen it up, but not bring it to a boil. Pour the hot nectar into your blender full of almond meal, followed immediately by the flower water if using, almond extract, and salt. Blend thoroughly, scraping down the sides of the work bowl as needed, until the syrup is incorporated and the whole sticky mass is entirely smooth.

Scoop out the almond paste as quickly as possible, because it will continue to thicken as it cools and become increasingly difficult to remove from beneath the blades of your machine. Store the soft marzipan in an airtight container in the fridge. Chill for at least 8 hours before using, as it will continue to firm up as it cools. Stored this way, your homemade marzipan will keep for 1–2 weeks. For longer-term storage, stash the container in your freezer for 2–3 months; let it thaw out at room temperature overnight before using.

SWEETENER SUBSTITUTES

Few things are more frustrating than getting all psyched up to start baking right away and then discovering that you're missing some critical ingredient. But wait! Before you start pulling out your grocery bags, with just a little flexibility and a quick wit, you can whip up your own substitutes. Especially in the case of most sweeteners, no grocery trip required. It does help to have a fairly well-stocked pantry so there are alternatives to turn to, but most people have at least plain sugar on hand.

Confectioner's Sugar

1 Cup Granulated Sugar
1 Tablespoon Cornstarch

Simply toss both ingredients into your food processor and blend for about 5 minutes, until superfine and powdery. Wait a few minutes for the dust to settle before opening up the lid so that powder doesn't fly everywhere and coat your kitchen.

Makes 1 cup

Brown Sugar

1 Cup Granulated Sugar
1 Tablespoon Molasses

Just like you would for the confectioner's sugar, combine both ingredients in your food processor and blend, but only for about a minute or so until the mixture is an even brown color and no dry patches of white sugar remain. Be sure to store in an airtight container or else it will become hard over time, but you can also microwave it for a few seconds to soften it up a bit.

Makes 1 cup

Maple Syrup

Though no substitute could fully replicate the delicate and incomparable flavor of pure maple syrup, I find that there is some wiggle room when it's going to be baked, and not quite as pure and singular when tasted. Save the real quality stuff for your pancakes and waffles, but you can get away with a little swap out here in your cakes.

If you've never experimented with fenugreek, you may be surprised to discover that it has an aroma reminiscent of maple syrup! To enhance maple sweets, try throwing in a tiny pinch of ground fenugreek right before baking.

1½ Cups Granulated Sugar
½ Cup Light Brown Sugar, Firmly Packed
1 Cup Water
2 Teaspoons Maple Extract

Place both sugars and the water in a medium saucepan over moderate heat, and simmer, stirring every now and then, until the sugar has fully dissolved. Bring to a boil and let bubble furiously for about 2–3 minutes, and then remove the pot from the heat. Stir in the maple extract. Let cool and store in a glass bottle at room temperature. If it crystallizes over time, simply reheat in the same manner until the crystals are dissolved back into the syrup.

Light Agave Nectar

Okay, you got me—this is essentially just a basic simple syrup recipe, no more exotic than regular old table sugar itself. While it's not appropriate for those with diabetes (and agave can sometimes be), it can easily fill the gap if you just want to get baking and get on with life. Golden syrup, if available, and light corn syrup can also fit the bill quite nicely.

2 Cups Granulated Sugar
1 Cup Water

Place both ingredients in a medium saucepan over moderate heat, and simmer, stirring every now and then, until the sugar has fully dissolved. Turn off the heat, let cool, and store in a glass bottle at room temperature. If it crystallizes over time, simply reheat in the same manner until the crystals are dissolved back into the syrup.

Makes 2 cups

VANILLA WAFER COOKIE CRUMBS

Makes about 4 cups of crumbs

¼ Cup Non-Dairy Margarine
¼ Cup Vegetable Shortening
1 Cup Granulated Sugar
2½ Cups All-Purpose Flour

¼ Teaspoon Baking Powder
¼ Teaspoon Salt
1½ Teaspoons Vanilla Extract
¼ Cup Plain Non-Dairy Milk

Preheat your oven to 350°F and line two baking sheets with Silpats or parchment paper.

In your stand mixer, cream together the margarine, shortening, and sugar, until completely smooth and homogeneous. Add in the flour, baking powder, salt, and vanilla, starting the mixer at a low speed so as not to toss the dry ingredients out. The mix will still seem a bit dry, so add in 1 tablespoon of non-dairy milk at a time letting the mixer process that each addition thoroughly, until it comes together in a cohesive dough. Use your hands to form it into a ball, and then divide that in half. Lay each half out on one Silpat and lightly coat the tops with flour. Use a rolling pin to flatten the dough down to about ⅛ inch thick. Take a pizza roller and slice the dough vertically and horizontally at about 1-inch intervals. No need to be precise here, these cuts just help the dough to cook more evenly and become crisp all over.

Bake each sheet individually, for about 14–18 minutes, until golden brown around the edges and firm in the center. The cookies will continue to firm up and become more crisp as they cool, but if you find that some pieces are still soft, just pop them back into the oven for an additional 5 minutes or so.

Once both sheets are baked and cooled, break them up and give them a spin in your food processor to create even crumbs. Store at room temperature in an airtight container until ready to use.

WHIPPED CREAM

Makes 2 cups

1½ Cups Coconut Milk
½ Cup Plain Soy or Coconut
    Creamer
6 Tablespoons Granulated Sugar

2 Tablespoons Agar-agar Flakes, or 2
    Teaspoons Powder
½ Teaspoon Vanilla Extract

In a medium saucepan, whisk together the coconut milk, soy cream, and sugar. Sprinkle the agar over the top and whisk vigorously to incorporate, being sure not to leave any lumps. Turn the stove up to medium heat and cook until the mixture comes to a full boil, stirring gently from time to time. Remove the pan from the heat and whisk in the vanilla. Cool to room temperature before stashing it in the fridge. Thoroughly chill for at least 3 hours, until completely solid—you should be able to turn the entire pot upside down and nothing will fall out (but don't hold it like that for too long, just in case!).

Scrape the disk of solidified whipped cream out of the pan and into your food processor or blender. Thoroughly purée, scraping down the sides and bottom of the bowl, until completely smooth. At first, it will seem dry and grainy, but just give the machine enough time to work out the lumps. Once silky and soft, dollop it onto desserts with a spoon or move it into a piping bag to give it a more "polished" look. This whipped cream is also stable at room temperature, meaning that it won't melt or weep like traditional whipped cream, so you can use it to frost or fill cakes too.

FOOD ALLERGY INDEX

Always check that the ingredients you are purchasing are safe for the food allergy or sensitivity in question. While I can note which recipes do not contain a particular allergen ingredient to the best of my knowledge, it is always up to the consumer to verify ingredients and any potential cross-contamination issues.

*Some of these recipes contain oats and/or oat flour, which are gluten-free provided that you seek out oats that are officially certified as such. Some individuals may still have a sensitivity to oats, however, so if you're unsure, quinoa flakes or flour can also be substituted.

**Several of my recipes contain non-dairy margarine as the only soy-based ingredient. While there are a few brands of soy-free margarine and shortening available internationally, I have not specifically trialed them in these recipes, and thus hesitate to recommend the swap. However, feel free to experiment if you are seeking more soy-free options.

**Simply select a non-dairy milk that is soy-free when called for in these recipes. Additionally, opt to use coconut creamer, coconut yogurt, and/or coconut oil where the option is given.

INDEX